HMH | into Reading™

W9-BFR-242

my Book

Grade 2

Modules 7–10

Authors and Advisors

Alma Flor Ada • Kylene Beers • F. Isabel Campoy
Joyce Armstrong Carroll • Nathan Clemens
Anne Cunningham • Martha C. Hougen • Tyrone C. Howard
Elena Izquierdo • Carol Jago • Erik Palmer
Robert E. Probst • Shane Templeton • Julie Washington

Contributing Consultants

David Dockterman • Jill Eggleton

Printed in the U.S.A.

ISBN   978-0-358-46152-4

4 5 6 7 8 9 10   0877   29 28 27 26 25 24 23 22

4500845361

r1.21

Everyone Has a Story

🌐 **SOCIAL STUDIES CONNECTION:** Important People 2

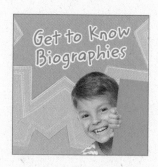

Get to Know Biographies 6
OPINION ESSAY

I Am Helen Keller 8
by Brad Meltzer • illustrated by Christopher Eliopoulos
BIOGRAPHY

How to Make a Timeline 40
by Boyd N. Gillin
PROCEDURAL TEXT

The Stories He Tells: The Story of Joseph Bruchac 50

by James Bruchac • illustrations by Brendan Kearney

BIOGRAPHY

Drum Dream Girl 64

by Margarita Engle • illustrated by Rafael López

POETRY

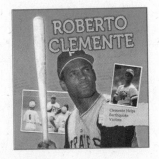

Roberto Clemente 90

MEDIA: VIDEO

Let's Wrap Up! 94

MODULE 8

Time to Grow!

🌱 **SCIENCE CONNECTION:** Plants... 96

The Growth of a Sunflower............ 100
PHOTO ESSAY

Experiment with What a Plant Needs to Grow 102
by Nadia Higgins
INFORMATIONAL TEXT

Jack and the Beanstalk..................... 116
by Helen Lester • illustrated by Jesús Aguado
FAIRY TALE

Jackie and the Beanstalk 130

by Lori Mortensen • illustrated by Ben Scruton

FAIRY TALE

Don't Touch Me! 144

by Elizabeth Preston

INFORMATIONAL TEXT

George Washington Carver: The Wizard of Tuskegee 154

by StoryBots

MEDIA: VIDEO

Let's Wrap Up! 158

MODULE 9

Home Sweet Habitat

🌿 **SCIENCE CONNECTION:** Animal Habitats 160

The Best Habitat for Me 164
OPINION ESSAY

The Long, Long Journey 166
by Sandra Markle • illustrated by Mia Posada
INFORMATIONAL TEXT

Sea Otter Pups 184
by Ruth Owen
INFORMATIONAL TEXT

At Home in the Wild 198
POETRY and SONG

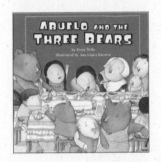

Abuelo and the Three Bears 212
by Jerry Tello • illustrated by Ana López Escrivá
FOLKTALE

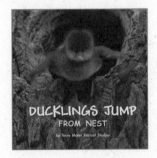

Ducklings Jump from Nest 232
by Terra Mater Factual Studios
MEDIA: VIDEO

Let's Wrap Up! 236

MODULE 10

Many Cultures, One World

🌐 **SOCIAL STUDIES CONNECTION:** World Cultures 238

Hello, World! 242
INFORMATIONAL TEXT

Where on Earth Is My Bagel? 244
by Frances and Ginger Park • illustrated by Grace Lin
REALISTIC FICTION

May Day Around the World 268
by Tori Telfer • illustrated by Lynne Avril
NARRATIVE NONFICTION

Goal!...278

by Sean Taylor • photographs by Caio Vilela

INFORMATIONAL TEXT

Poems in the Attic.............................292

by Nikki Grimes • illustrated by Elizabeth Zunon

POETRY

What's for Lunch
Around the World?.............................314

MEDIA: VIDEO

Let's Wrap Up!...................................318

Glossary...320

Index of Titles and Authors...........330

Everyone Has a Story

"He who is not courageous enough to take risks will accomplish nothing in life."

—Muhammad Ali

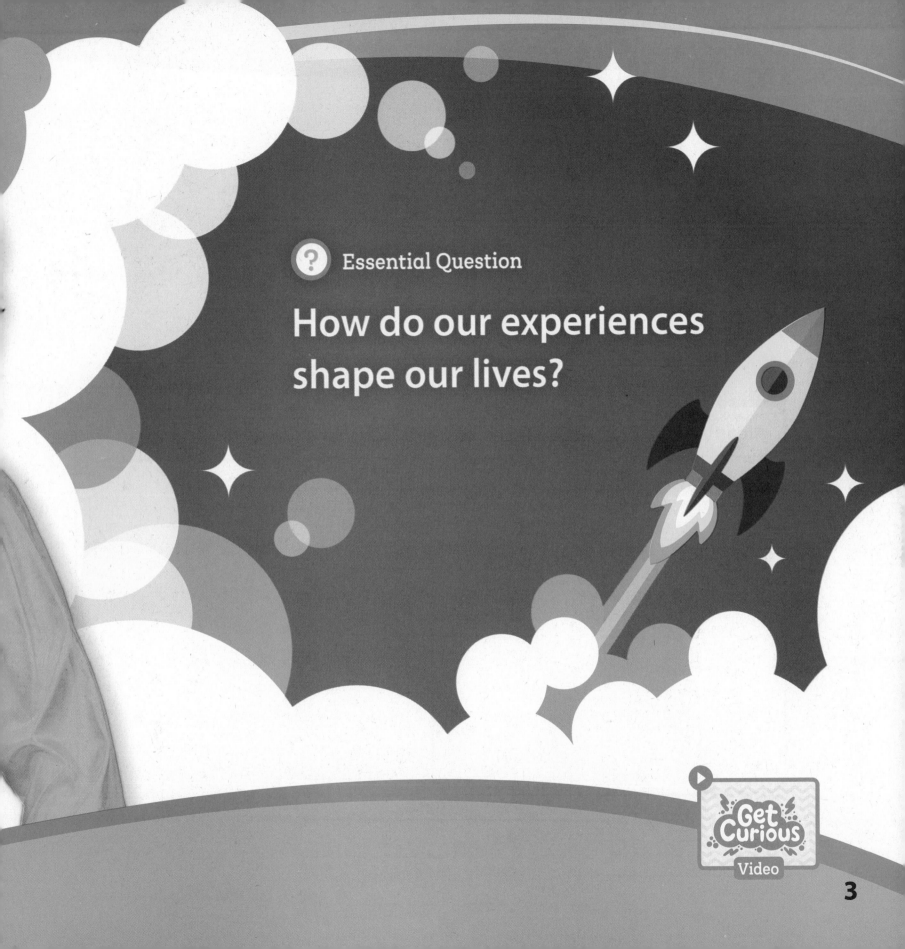

? Essential Question

How do our experiences shape our lives?

Get Curious Video

3

Words About Important People

Complete the Vocabulary Network to show what you know
about the words.

account

Meaning: An **account** is a report of something that happened.

Synonyms and Antonyms	**Drawing**

achieve

Meaning: When you **achieve** something, you get it after a lot of hard work.

Synonyms and Antonyms	Drawing

hurdle

Meaning: A **hurdle** is a problem that could stop you from doing something.

Synonyms and Antonyms	Drawing

Get to Know Biographies

Biographies are a type of informational text. They tell about real people's lives.

Alex wrote his opinion about biographies to share with his class.

Alex Lewis
2nd Grade

The Elements of a Biography

- ☑ Important dates and events
- ☑ Place of birth
- ☑ Childhood and family information
- ☑ Problems or challenges
- ☑ Why the person is important

Why I Like Reading Biographies

by Alex Lewis

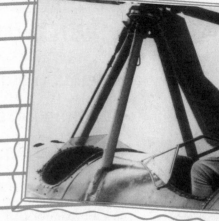

I think biographies are the best kind of book. You can learn so much from them! I like to read them to learn about real people and about history.

I read a biography about the pilot Amelia Earhart. I learned how much she did in her life! She bought her first airplane only a few months after her first flying lesson. In 1932, she became the first woman to fly by herself across the Atlantic Ocean.

I like that biographies can teach us so many different things. I learned about civil rights when I read about Dr. Martin Luther King, Jr. I read about the ways Dr. King helped people get the same rights.

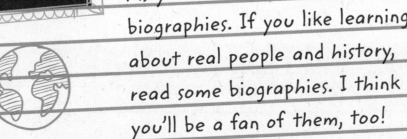

As you can tell, I love biographies. If you like learning about real people and history, read some biographies. I think you'll be a fan of them, too!

7

Prepare to Read

GENRE STUDY **Biographies** tell about real people's lives. As you read *I Am Helen Keller*, look for:

- events in order from earliest to latest
- information about why this person is important
- ways the person has made a difference

SET A PURPOSE Read to find out the most important ideas in each part. Then **synthesize,** or put together these ideas in your mind, to find out what the text really means to you.

POWER WORDS

deal

figured

communicate

motioned

approached

series

selfless

potential

Meet Brad Meltzer.

I Am
Helen Keller

by Brad Meltzer

illustrated by Christopher Eliopoulos

I am **Helen Keller**.

When I was little, I was just like you.
I loved to play.
I loved my dog.
And I loved seeing all the bright beautiful flowers.
I also loved copying people. At six months old,
I could already say . . .

On the day I turned one, I started walking.
Oh, and there was another word I always loved.

Just like any other kid, right?
But there's one thing that made me different.
When I was nineteen months old, I got very sick.
The doctors said I wouldn't live.
I did live, but the sickness made me blind and deaf.

This is how I see the world.

Close your eyes and block your ears.
I couldn't see anything.
Or hear anything.

That's right.
Nothing.

I know it seems scary.

It was scary for me too.

Back then, people didn't know how to deal with someone who was deaf and blind.

My relatives thought I was a monster.

They were right: I wasn't well-behaved. I was extremely frustrated. In my dark world, I couldn't tell if anyone noticed me or cared about me.

I couldn't see or hear what I was doing.

14

But by the time I was five, I'd figured out small ways to communicate.
To say YES, I nodded my head.
For NO, I shook it from side to side.

To say FATHER, I motioned
to put on his glasses.

For MOTHER, I rested
my hand on my face.

For baby sister,
I did this. . .

And when I'd shiver like I
was cold, it really meant. . .

But even with those sighs, I couldn't get my dog, Belle, to play with me.

I didn't know how to speak, so I couldn't call her.

I just wanted to play with my dog.

The saddest part was, I got used to a dark and silent world.

People told my parents to give up on me. That I'd never be good at anything.

They didn't listen, though.

After reading about another blind and deaf girl, my parents found something they hadn't had since I'd gotten sick.

Hope.

We *all* do.

Everyone needs a teacher.

Still, I had no idea what the world was about to bring me.

I never had a more important day.
I was six years old.
From the way my mother was hurrying, I knew something big was coming.
I stood on the porch, waiting, feeling the sun on my face.

Someone approached—I could feel footsteps.
I reached out, thinking it was my mother.
She pulled me into her arms.

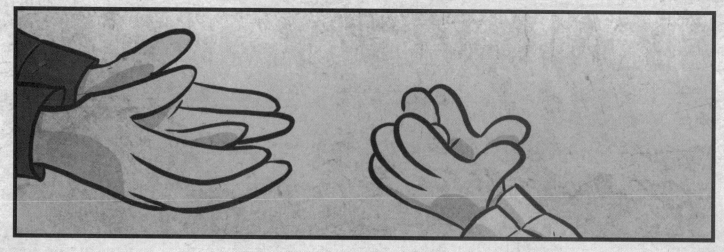

Her name was
Anne Sullivan.
She's the teacher
who changed my life.

19

In one of her first lessons, she gave me a toy doll.

After letting me play with it, she spelled the word DOLL into the palm of my hand.

D-O-L-L.

CAN YOU FEEL THE LETTERS?

D-O-L-L.

I could feel them.

But I didn't know what letters or words were. Or how they worked.

It didn't stop Miss Sullivan.

One day, we were arguing as she was trying to teach me the words MUG and WATER.

I got so upset, I took my new doll and smashed it on the ground.

I got angry a lot back then.

It was so hard for me.

I was frustrated.

Never losing her patience, my teacher took me outside.
At a nearby spout, she put my hand under the
running water.
In my other hand, she spelled the word.
W-A-T-E-R.

W-A-T-E-R.

From there, I realized that everything had a name.
Every object I touched seemed to burst to life.

And now, when I wrote words in my teacher's hand,
I had someone who could understand me.

When you're learning something new, it's often hard.
I started with words.
My vocabulary grew fast.
Eventually, I learned the meaning of the word LOVE.
I had given my teacher some flowers. So she spelled into my hand . . .

I LOVE HELEN.

Confused, I asked her . . . WHAT IS LOVE?

"It is here," she spelled while tapping at my heart.
I was still confused.
It was hard to understand something I couldn't touch.

It made no sense. Why couldn't my teacher show me love? But then, she explained . . .

YOU CAN'T TOUCH CLOUDS, BUT YOU CAN FEEL RAIN AND KNOW HOW HAPPY FLOWERS ARE TO GET WATERED.

THAT IS HOW LOVE IS.

YOU CAN'T TOUCH LOVE, BUT YOU CAN FEEL HOW HAPPY IT MAKES YOU.

There, in that moment, my whole world changed.
It was as if there were invisible lines that stretched between me and everyone else in my life.
Close your eyes.
You can feel it too—your connection to your family and friends.

26

Still, life was never easy.
Without sight, I couldn't see people's faces.
Without sound, I couldn't hear their voices.
But one of my greatest breakthroughs came when
I learned to do what you're doing right now.
Reading.

To practice, I'd match each word with its object and make sentences.
This was my favorite game.
We played it for hours.
See if you can find the sentence: Girl is in wardrobe.

From there, I started reading real books.
Just like you.
The only difference was, my books were in
Braille, which is a series of raised dots that you
read with your fingers.
These dots spell my name. H-E-L-E-N.

Want to read your name in
Braille? Here's the alphabet.

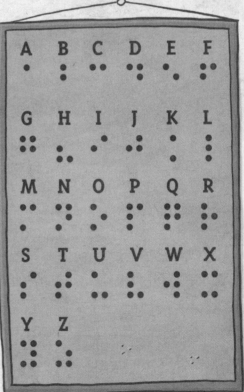

To make reading even more fun, my teacher took me outside.

She knew I loved feeling the sun on my face and smelling the pine needles.

I read my books so many times, I wore down the raised dots.

There were *The Arabian Nights*, *Robinson Crusoe*, and one of my favorites, *Little Women*.

In those pages, I met brave boys and girls who could hear and see.

"I AM NOT AFRAID OF STORMS, FOR I AM LEARNING HOW TO SAIL MY SHIP."

One of Miss Sullivan's best lessons came when she showed how plants grow.

FEEL THESE BUDS.

SOME BUDS OPEN FAST.

OTHERS OPEN SLOWLY.

A FLOWER CAN ONLY BLOOM IF IT'S WATERED.

When I was nine years old, I wanted to learn how to speak. Even Miss Sullivan was worried about teaching me. She thought I'd get frustrated. But nothing would stop me now.

To help me, Miss Sullivan took me to a teacher named Sarah Fuller, who would put my hand to her face and let me feel her tongue and lips as she made each sound.

In an hour, I learned the letters M, P, A, S, T and I.

Now I could call my dog, and she'd come to me.

At my seventh lesson, I spoke this sentence, the one sentence that I'd repeat over and over:

As I got older, I didn't just learn to speak English. I learned French and German.

For college, I wanted to go to Radcliffe, at Harvard University.

At Harvard, most of my books weren't available in Braille, so Miss Sullivan spelled out many of the textbooks in my hand. That's how much I loved learning. And that's how patient and selfless Miss Sullivan was.

I became the first deaf and blind person to earn a college degree.
I wouldn't be the last.
As I grew older, I wrote twelve books and visited thirty-four countries.
But the most important thing I did was to make sure that other
people with disabilities could get the same education I had.

In my life, they said I was different. They said I'd never be normal. But the truth is, there's no such thing as a "normal" life.

Every one of us is like a flower that must be watered. Every one of us is full of potential.

And every one of us can overcome obstacles.

Look at me.

Hear my words.

I may not be able to see, but I have vision.

I may not be able to hear, but I have a voice.

34

Think of your life as a hill that must be climbed.

There's no correct path to get to the top.

We all zigzag in our own ways.

At some point, you'll slip,

      you'll fall,

         you'll tumble back down again.

But if you get back up and keep climbing, I promise you . . .

You will reach the top.

Don't let anything hold you back.
Our lives are what we make of them.
There will always be obstacles.
But there will always be ways around them.

I am Helen Keller
and I won't let anything stop me.

Use details from *I Am Helen Keller* to answer these questions with a partner.

1. **Synthesize** Why do you think Helen Keller's life still inspires people today?

2. Who is telling the story? Why do you think the author chose to write the text this way?

3. Why is learning to spell *water* a very important event in Helen's life?

Talking Tip

Be polite. Wait for your turn to talk. Then tell your idea to your partner.

I think that _____.

Write a Life Lesson

PROMPT What is the most important life lesson you learned from *I Am Helen Keller*? How can that lesson be helpful to you and to others? Use details from the text and pictures to explain your ideas.

PLAN First, write the life lesson in the top of the chart. Then, write three reasons why you think the lesson is important.

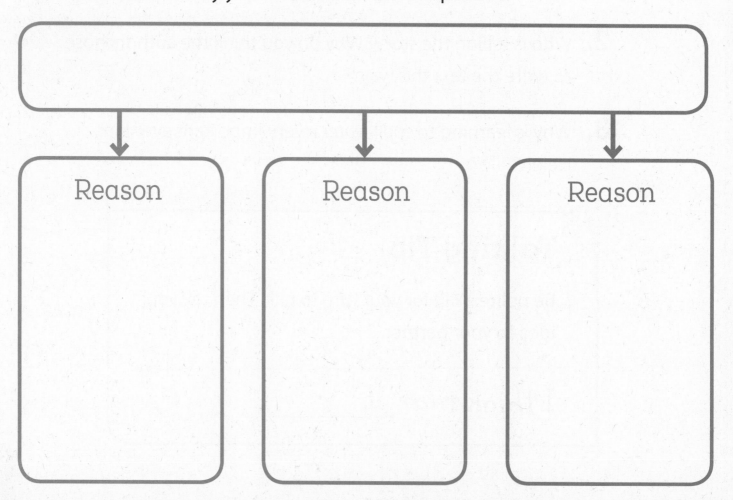

Reason

Reason

Reason

WRITE Now write sentences that describe the life lesson you learned. Explain why you think that lesson can be helpful to you and to others. Remember to:

- Use *because* to connect your reasons to your opinions.

- Use language that shows your feelings about the lesson.

_____

_____

_____

_____

_____

_____

_____

_____

_____

Prepare to Read

GENRE STUDY **Procedural texts** tell readers how to do or make something. When you read *How to Make a Timeline*, notice:

- directions for readers to follow
- a list of materials needed for the project
- the model, or picture of what the final project will look like
- steps that show order

SET A PURPOSE As you read, stop and think if you don't understand something. Reread, ask yourself questions, use what you already know, and look for visual clues to help you understand the text.

POWER WORDS

timeline

statements

arrange

current

Build Background: Parts of a Timeline

How to Make a
TIMELINE

by Boyd N. Gillin

BIOGRAPHY

A biography tells about the events in a real person's life. It takes time to read a full biography because it has many details and is full of stories.

A biography takes time to read.

THE LIFE OF JOHN HANCOCK

1737	1754	1775
January 23: Born in Braintree, Massachusetts	Graduated from Harvard College	**May 24:** Became president of Congress

TIMELINE

Another way to share information about a person's life is through a timeline. A timeline uses visuals and dates to show a sequence of events at a glance. Because of this, a timeline doesn't have a lot of words on it. You read a timeline from left to right, just like a sentence.

Anyone can make a timeline! A person doesn't have to be famous or a grown-up. Everyone's life is filled with special events.

A timeline gives a lot of information with just a quick glance.

1776

July 4: First person to sign Declaration of Independence

1780

Elected Governor of Massachusetts

43

Tramayne's TIMELINE

Tramayne made a timeline of his life. Read the statements he wrote. What ideas can you get from Tramayne's timeline to make one about your own life?

To make a timeline about *your* life, think about events from the past that are special to you.

Feb. 13, 2012

Born in Dallas, Texas

2016

Became a big brother

Spring 2018

Received an award from the library

For example, when were you born? What exciting things have happened to you? Have you won an award or learned a new skill? Write down the dates of important events in your life. If you need help thinking of events or dates, ask family members. You might even learn more about yourself! Let's get started!

Summer 2018
Started taking photography class

Oct. 25, 2018
Started taking trumpet lessons

2019
Helped to plant a tree

CREATE YOUR OWN!

Look back at Tramayne's timeline. Use it as a model to create your own.

1. Write important events from your life on notecards. Put the date at the top of the card, and write what happened at the bottom. Leave space for a picture!

2. Arrange all of your notecards in order. Put the earliest event on top and the most recent event on the bottom.

3. Add drawings or pictures to your notecards. You can use photographs if your parents say it is okay.

4. Add your notecards to a piece of string with clothespins or paper clips. Put the earliest event on the left and the most current one on the right.

5. Share your timeline with the class. It will be fun to tell your friends about yourself.

Use details from *How to Make a Timeline* to answer these questions with a partner.

1. **Monitor and Clarify** What did you do when you came to a part of the text that you didn't understand? Tell how it helped or didn't help you.

2. Why did the author number the steps on page 46?

3. How do the headings and symbols help you to find and understand information in this text?

Talking Tip

Use details from the text to explain your ideas. Complete the sentence below.

I think _____ because _____.

Write an Explanation

PROMPT Choose one event from your timeline. What makes this memory special to you? Explain why it belongs on a timeline about you.

PLAN First, explain why this memory is special to you.

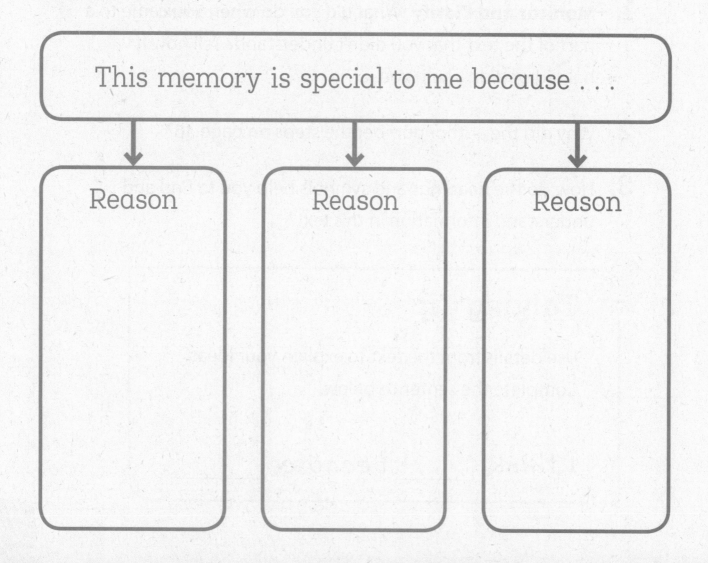

This memory is special to me because . . .

Reason

Reason

Reason

WRITE Now write an explanation to tell why you chose this event for your timeline. Describe why it is important to you. Remember to:

- Include details that tell what you did and how you felt.

- Use details from *How to Make a Timeline* to explain why this event belongs on your timeline.

_____

_____

_____

_____

_____

_____

_____

_____

_____

Prepare to Read

GENRE STUDY ▸ **Biographies** tell about real people's lives. As you read *The Stories He Tells: The Story of Joseph Bruchac,* notice:

- details and events in the person's life
- events in order from earliest to latest
- photos of the person

SET A PURPOSE ▸ Read to make smart guesses, or **inferences,** about things the author does not say. Use clues in the text and pictures to help you.

POWER WORDS

ashamed

elders

overflowing

pride

**Meet
James Bruchac.**

THE STORIES HE TELLS

The Story of Joseph Bruchac

by James Bruchac • illustrations by Brendan Kearney

Joseph Bruchac III was born on October 16, 1942. He was born in Saratoga Springs, New York. His parents' names were Joseph Jr. and Marion Flora Bowman. Joseph grew up in Greenfield Center, New York. That is in the foothills of the Adirondack Mountains.

Joseph in second grade

Joseph was raised by his mother's parents. His grandfather was an Abenaki Indian. He had a strong love for animals and nature. His grandmother was one of the first women to ever graduate from Albany Law School. She liked books and learning.

Albany Law School

Joseph's grandparents ran a small general store and gas station right next to the house where he grew up. The store was on one of the main roads into the Adirondack Mountains. As a boy, Joseph loved to hear all of the stories and tall tales told by the people who came into the store.

Joseph's family's general store

There were not many children out in the country where Joseph lived. Because of this, he often played by himself in the forest. Sometimes he would walk by Grandpa Jesse's side. Grandpa Jesse taught Joseph a lot about animals, nature, and gardening. He never spoke much about his Native American background. Grandpa Jesse and his family and other Native Americans had been treated badly.

Joseph and his grandfather

Grandpa Jesse said he left school when he was in fourth grade. Why? He was being called mean names. Hearing such family stories made Joseph feel sad. It also made him want to learn more. He wanted to learn the stories and traditions his grandfather was too **ashamed** to share.

Joseph's grandmother passed on to him a love of school. With this, Joseph went to college at Cornell University. While in college, he began to learn everything he could learn about Native American ways and beliefs. As an adult, Joseph traveled the country meeting Native American **elders**. These elders gladly shared their stories and traditions with him.

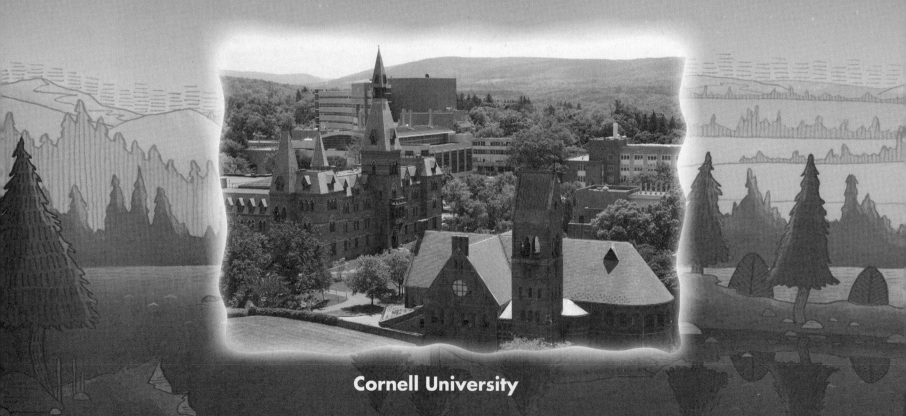

Cornell University

Joseph and his wife Carol met in college. They married and had two sons named James and Jesse. Joseph was **overflowing** with stories that he would often retell to his two sons.

Before long, Joseph began to share the stories with others outside the family. Times had changed a lot since Grandpa Jesse left school. Now when Joseph told the stories, people listened and were interested. They felt Joseph's retellings were important. They respected him. Joseph also began to write stories in books.

Joseph sharing stories

In just a few years, Joseph Bruchac became known all across the world as a Native American storyteller. He has won many awards for his storytelling. Joseph has also written more than 120 books of poetry, fiction, and nonfiction. Most of the books are about Native Americans.

Joseph connects with audiences around the world.

Growing up learning about Native American traditions, James and Jesse are also storytellers. Joseph's oldest son, James, is also a wilderness and tracking expert. His younger son, Jesse, teaches the Abenaki language.

James at work

Jesse, James, and Joseph Bruchac

59

Joseph still lives in the house where he grew up. He writes and shares stories almost every day. He takes extra pride in seeing a love for stories continue to his grandkids. He and his sons continue to help pass along these once hidden traditions to future generations!

Joseph and his grandchildren

Turn and Talk

Use details from *The Stories He Tells: The Story of Joseph Bruchac* to answer these questions with a partner.

1. **Make Inferences** Why is passing on traditions important to Joseph Bruchac? Use evidence from the text to explain your answer.

2. What is the central idea of this text?

3. Think about what the text and photos tell you about Joseph Bruchac. What qualities do you think a person needs to be a great storyteller?

Listening Tip

Listen carefully to your partner. Think of what you agree with and do not agree with.

Write a Letter

PROMPT What would you say in a letter to Joseph Bruchac?
What questions would you ask him? Think about which details in
the text were most interesting to you and made you curious.

PLAN First, list interesting facts you learned about Mr. Bruchac.
Then write questions you would like to ask him.

Facts	My Questions

WRITE Now write a letter to Joseph Bruchac. Ask him questions about his life and work. Tell which fact about his life is most interesting to you. Explain why. Remember to:

- Use commas in your greeting and closing.

- Begin your questions with *what, why, who, when,* or *how*.

_____

_____

_____

_____

_____

_____

_____

_____

_____

_____

Prepare to Read

GENRE STUDY **Poetry** uses images, sounds, and rhythm to express feelings. As you read *Drum Dream Girl,* look for:

- words that appeal to the senses
- words that make you think of powerful images or pictures
- words that describe

SET A PURPOSE As you read, **create mental images,** or make pictures in your mind, to help you understand details in the text.

POWER WORDS
secret
whir
reminding
dared
alone
deserved
starlit
allowed

Meet Margarita Engle.

DRUM DREAM GIRL

by **Margarita Engle**

illustrated by

Rafael López

On an island of music
in a city of drumbeats
the drum dream girl
dreamed

of pounding tall conga drums

tapping small *bongó* drums

and boom boom booming

with long, loud sticks

on big, round, silvery

moon-bright *timbales*.

But everyone

on the island of music

in the city of drumbeats

believed that only boys

should play drums

so the drum dream girl
had to keep dreaming
quiet
secret
drumbeat
dreams.

71

At outdoor cafés that looked like gardens

she heard drums played by men

but when she closed her eyes

she could also hear

her own imaginary

music.

When she walked under
wind-wavy palm trees
in a flower-bright park
she heard the whir of parrot wings
the clack of woodpecker beaks
the dancing tap
of her own footsteps
and the comforting pat
of her own
heartbeat.

73

At carnivals, she listened
to the rattling beat
of towering
dancers
on stilts

and the dragon clang
of costumed drummers
wearing huge masks.

75

At home, her fingertips
rolled out their own
dreamy drum rhythm
on tables and chairs . . .

76

and even though everyone

kept reminding her that girls

on the island of music

had never played drums

the brave drum dream girl
dared to play
tall conga drums
small *bongó* drums
and big, round, silvery
moon-bright *timbales*.

Her hands seemed to fly

as they rippled

rapped

and pounded

all the rhythms

of her drum dreams.

79

Her big sisters were so excited

that they invited her to join

their new all-girl dance band

80

but their father said only boys

should play drums.

So the drum dream girl

had to keep dreaming

and drumming

alone

82

until finally
her father offered
to find a music teacher
who could decide if her drums
deserved
to be heard.

The drum dream girl's
teacher was amazed.
The girl knew so much
but he taught her more
and more
and more

and she practiced
and she practiced
and she practiced

until the teacher agreed

that she was ready

to play her small *bongó* drums

outdoors at a starlit café

that looked like a garden

85

where everyone who heard
her dream-bright music
sang
and danced
and decided
that girls should always
be allowed to play
drums

and both girls and boys
should feel free
to dream.

86

Turn and Talk

Use details from *Drum Dream Girl* to answer these questions with a partner.

1. **Create Mental Images** What does the drum dream girl dream about? Which of the poem's words help you picture it in your mind?

2. What does the drum dream girl do when her father says only boys play drums? What does that tell you about her?

3. What is the poet's message?

Talking Tip

Answer your partner's questions. Explain your ideas clearly.

I mean that _____.

Write a Journal Entry

PROMPT How would the drum dream girl describe her first concert at the starlit café? What did she see, hear, and feel? Use details from the text and illustrations to explain your answer.

PLAN First, fill in the web with four details about the concert.

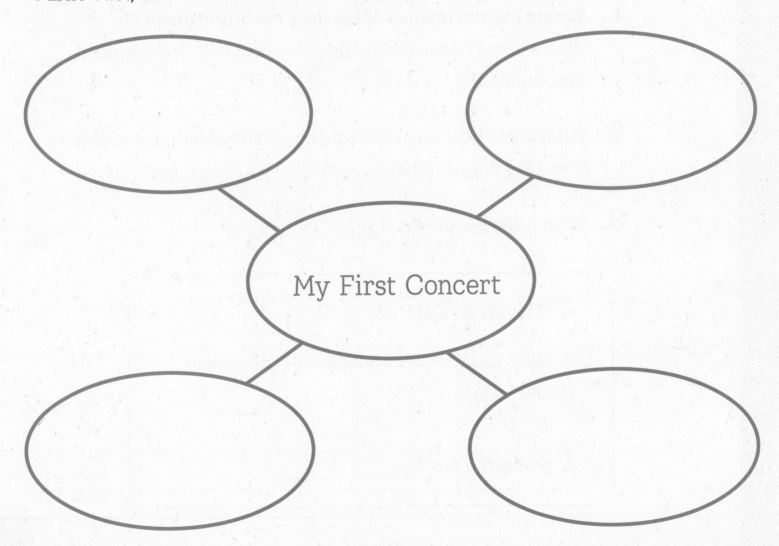

My First Concert

WRITE Now write a journal entry from the drum dream girl's point of view that describes the night of the concert. Remember to:

- Use what you know about the drum dream girl to explain how she feels that night.

- Use the words *I* and *me* to tell the story as she would.

_____

_____

_____

_____

_____

_____

_____

_____

_____

Prepare to View

GENRE STUDY **Videos** are short movies that give you information or something for you to watch for enjoyment. As you watch *Roberto Clemente,* notice:

- how pictures, sounds, and words work together
- what the video is about
- how the video makes you feel
- the tone or mood of the video

SET A PURPOSE When others want to persuade you to agree with an idea, they give reasons to support it. Pay attention to the ideas and opinions in the video. Listen for facts and reasons that support them. What does the narrator want you to think or believe about Roberto Clemente?

Build Background: Baseball

ROBERTO CLEMENTE

Clemente Helps
Earthquake
Victims

As You View As you watch the video, listen to the words carefully. Look for evidence that shows what type of person Roberto Clemente was. Think about whether the video is trying to make you think or feel a certain way.

Use details from *Roberto Clemente* to answer these questions
with a partner.

1. **Ideas and Support** The narrator says that Roberto
   Clemente was a kind, caring man. Which details in the video
   support that opinion?

2. In your own words, describe the important events in
   Roberto Clemente's life in the order they happened.

3. What is the central idea of the video? What does the narrator
   want you to think and feel?

Talking Tip

Wait for your turn to speak. Tell about your
feelings and ideas clearly.

I feel that _____.

Let's Wrap Up!

(?) Essential Question

How do our experiences shape our lives?

· ·

**Pick one of these activities to show what you have learned
about the topic.**

1. Biographies Rule!

Think about the texts you have read. What makes a great
biography? Using details from the texts, write
six rules a writer should follow to write a
great biography.

Word Challenge

Can you use the
word achieve in
your rules?

2. Show a Lesson

Create a poster that shares a life lesson you learned from one of the texts. Think about how words, colors, designs, or pictures can grab someone's attention and make him or her think. Share your poster with a group. Explain why you think that lesson is important.

My Notes

Time to Grow!

"The secret garden bloomed and bloomed
and every morning revealed new miracles."

—Frances Hodgson Burnett

What do plants need to live and grow?

Get Curious Video

Words About Plants

Complete the Vocabulary Network to show what you know about the words.

fertilize

Meaning: When you **fertilize** soil, you add something that helps plants grow.

Synonyms and Antonyms	Drawing

germinate

Meaning: Seeds **germinate** when they begin to grow.

Synonyms and Antonyms	Drawing

survive

Meaning: When things **survive**, they stay alive.

Synonyms and Antonyms	Drawing

THE GROWTH OF A SUNFLOWER

A **photo essay** is a group of photographs that tells a story or explains something. The photos may be paired with text, too. Look at the photos and read the captions to learn how a plant grows.

1

2

3

Find a large pot with holes in the bottom. Fill the pot with soil and then plant the seed.

Cover the seed with soil. Add water and sun.

After a few days, the seed germinates, or begins to grow. Give the seedling water and sun. This keeps it growing. You can fertilize it, too.

5

BLOOM!

4

As the bud opens, the flower begins to form.

The young plant grows taller. Be sure it still gets water and sunlight. Soon, a bud starts to develop.

Prepare to Read

GENRE STUDY **Informational text** is nonfiction. It gives facts about a topic. As you read *Experiment with What a Plant Needs to Grow*, pay attention to:

- photos with labels
- order of events
- cause and effect
- ways that pictures and words help readers understand the text

SET A PURPOSE As you read, **make connections** to other texts you have read about the topic. Find ways that they are the same and different. This will help you understand and remember each text.

POWER WORDS

minerals

fuels

process

provides

sprout

moisten

seedlings

spiky

Meet Nadia Higgins.

Experiment with What a Plant Needs to Grow

by
Nadia Higgins

What Are Plants?

Plants are living things. They grow. They reproduce. Like you, plants need air and water. They need minerals to stay healthy. They also need food.

For a plant, food starts with sunlight. Sunlight fuels photosynthesis. This is a process in which green leaves make food using air and water.

With enough sunlight and water, flowering plants will bloom.

Plants give us food, wood, and medicine. Photosynthesis provides the oxygen we need to breathe!

Can Seeds Get Too Much Water?

Water helps a plant stay strong and sturdy. But even before a plant shoots out of the ground, its seeds need water to sprout.

Can seeds get too much water? Let's find out.

Plants die if they don't get enough water.

What you need:

three small bowls

water

handful of grass seeds

six cotton balls

pencil and paper

Steps:

1. Start by putting two cotton balls in each of the bowls.

2. Next, fill the first bowl so the cotton balls are covered with water. Moisten the second bowl's cotton balls all the way through. Don't add any water to the third bowl.

3. Sprinkle about a dozen seeds on top of the cotton balls in each bowl.

Very Wet

A little Wet

Dry

Label the bowls so you remember which is which.

Keep checking your **seedlings** for a week.
Which sprouts are the tallest and sturdiest?

4. Put the cotton balls in a sunny place.

5. Check the bowls every day. Make sure the first two cotton balls stay covered in water. Make sure the second two stay moist.

After a few days, some seeds will sprout.

107

Think It Through

A seed has a coat that protects it. Water softens the coat, so the seed can sprout. But seeds also need air. Too much water can keep a seed from getting enough air.

Horse chestnuts have **spiky** seed coats to protect their seeds.

Now Try This

Plants need minerals to be healthy. Most plants get minerals from the soil. Predict how long your grass can survive without soil. Watch the grass sprouts to see if you were right.

Be sure to write down your prediction before you start experimenting.

How Do Leaves Get Air?

We just saw that seeds need air to sprout. Roots need air, too. Air is also part of photosynthesis.

As they make food, green leaves take air in and let it out. Let's find out how.

You can easily poke your finger into good garden soil. The loose soil holds lots of tiny spaces. Those air-filled spaces keep roots healthy.

What you need:

petroleum jelly

leafy green plant

camera

masking tape

Steps:

1. Spread a heavy coat of petroleum jelly over the tops of five leaves of your plant.

2. Do the same on the undersides of five other leaves.

3. Put your plant in a sunny window. Then take its picture.

4. Observe your plant every day for the next week.

Mark the tops of the coated leaves with tape so you can easily find them again.

Compare what you see to the photo you took on the first day.

How are the leaves different from your photo?

Think It Through

Petroleum jelly kept some of the leaves from letting air in and out. Those leaves started to wilt. The leaves that were coated on the bottom wilted the most.

Measure Like a Scientist

Measuring helps scientists show exactly what is happening. Let's look at some ways you might use measuring in a plant experiment.

Measurement	Test	Tool	Unit (metric)
Weight	Weigh two seeds. Is one heavier?	Scale	Ounces (grams)
Length	Measure a bean seedling in the morning. Then measure it the next day. Did it grow taller?	Ruler	Inches (centimeters)
Time	Track how many days it takes for a plant to bloom.	Calendar	Days
Volume	Measure how much water you are adding to a pot.	Measuring cup	Cup (milliliters)

 **Turn** and **Talk**

Use details from *Experiment with What a Plant Needs to Grow* to answer these questions with a partner.

1. **Make Connections** Think about *Experiment with What a Plant Needs to Grow* and *The Growth of a Sunflower*. Compare and contrast what each text taught you about plants.

2. How do the captions and labels on pages 106 and 107 help you understand the experiment?

3. Some pages have numbered steps and some do not. Why did the author organize the text this way?

Talking Tip

Use details from the text to explain your ideas. Complete the sentence below.

I think _____ because _____.

Write a Lab Report

PROMPT Imagine you are conducting one of the experiments in the text. What observations would you make? What conclusions could you draw? Use details from the text and photos to explain your ideas.

PLAN First, write or draw what you would see at the beginning of the experiment. Next, write or draw what you would see at the end of the experiment.

Beginning

End

WRITE Now write three observations you would make during the experiment. Then write a conclusion you can make from your observations. Remember to:

- Use details from the text to describe what you see and do.

- Use words such as *first, then,* and *next* to tell the order of your observations.

_____

_____

_____

_____

_____

_____

_____

_____

_____

Prepare to Read

GENRE STUDY ▶ **Fairy tales** are old stories that have made-up characters and events that could not happen. As you read *Jack and the Beanstalk,* look for:

- the beginning, middle, and ending of the story
- characters who are not found in real life
- an ending that is happy
- storytelling phrases (*once upon a time, happily ever after*)

SET A PURPOSE ▶ As you read, **retell** the story. Use your own words to tell what happens in the beginning, middle, and end of the story.

POWER WORDS

swipe

whacked

whimpered

plenty

Meet Helen Lester.

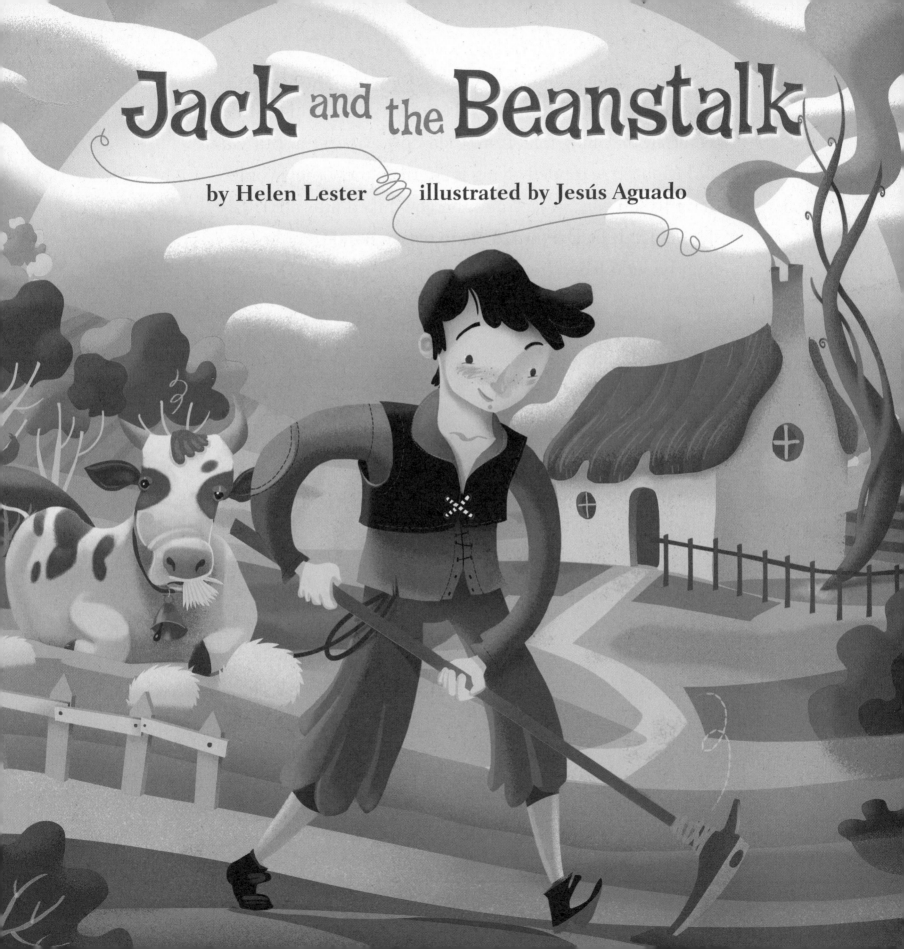

Jack and the Beanstalk

by Helen Lester   illustrated by Jesús Aguado

Once upon a time, a boy named Jack lived with his mother in a poor little hut. What money they had for food came from selling milk from their cow, Moozetta. But when old Moozetta stopped giving milk, they knew they would have to sell *her*. So Jack and the cow hiked into the village. Hours later, Jack returned alone with a handful of beans that he held like a treasure. *Beans*? Beans.

118

"You've got to be kidding me!" yelled Jack's mother.
"You were supposed to sell Moozetta for MONEY!
Those beans won't put food on the table!"

"But the beans are so pretty," said Jack.

"This is a mess," sighed his mother.

Jack went outside and planted the pretty beans in a
sunny spot. He gave them a drink of water. Maybe, just
maybe, they would grow. And grow they did!

Overnight, the seeds had sprouted. By morning, they had wound into a beautiful beanstalk.

"How did it grow so fast?" wondered Jack.

It had grown up…up…up and out of sight, beyond the clouds.

"WOWEE!" exclaimed Jack. Being a curious lad, he simply had to climb it.

Where would the beanstalk lead? He went up and up, higher and higher, until he went beyond the clouds.

GO AWAY!
ONLY GIANTS
ALLOWED!

BEWARE:
LARGE HUNGRY
BEINGS

Tada! Jack gazed upon an enormous castle.
He saw some creepy-looking signs, too.
From inside the castle a voice boomed,

"Fee-fi-fo-fum!
Time for beddy. Ho-dee-hum."

On the ground was a little bag of gold.

Jack looked left and right, and—SWIPE!—
down the beanstalk he went with his treasure. The
big sleeper surely wouldn't miss such a small bag.

At the sight of the gold, Jack's mother allowed
herself a smile.

The next morning, Jack climbed the beanstalk again.

"Fee-fi-fo-fum!
Time for beddy. Ho-dee-hum."

"Good timing," thought Jack, and this time he
helped himself to a goose who was very busy laying
golden eggs.

At the sight of the busy goose cranking out golden
eggs, Jack's mother allowed herself a giggle.

The next morning, Jack leapt up the beanstalk like a mountain goat. He was eager to find more treasure. Oh, dear. He would have to face the music.

"Fee-fi-fo-fum!
WHERE ON EARTH DID YOU COME FROM?"

"From down on Earth," replied Jack. "Well, I came up my beanstalk, which is IN earth. You see, I gave it sunshine, and water, and — "

But the giant was not interested in Jack's gardening skills. He was HUNGRY! Jack, being nimble and quick, hurried down the beanstalk.

As the giant followed and was halfway down, Jack grabbed an ax, whacked the beanstalk, and SPLAT.

"My toe hurts," whimpered the giant. "And how will I get home?"

"I'll show you," said Jack kindly. First, he showed the giant how to water the beanstalk. Together, they cared for the plant. It grew up and up beyond the clouds.

Now the giant could climb home, and Jack bought Moozetta back. He returned everything he had taken from the giant. The gentle giant told his new friends they could keep the goose.

From that day on, Jack, his mother, the goose, and Moozetta had plenty to eat and lived happily ever after.

Once in a while, they invited the giant down for a giant feast. These feasts always included plenty of leafy beanstalk greens.

Use details from *Jack and the Beanstalk* to answer these questions with a partner.

1. **Retell** In your own words, retell the most important story events in order.

2. On page 120, why does the author repeat the words *up* and *higher*? What is she trying to show the reader?

3. How do you think Jack felt when he first saw the giant? How do his feelings change? Use details from the text and pictures to explain your answer.

Listening Tip

Listen carefully and politely. Look at your partner to show you are paying attention.

Write a Dos and Don'ts List

PROMPT If you want to make friends with a giant, what should you do? What shouldn't you do? Use details from *Jack and the Beanstalk* and other stories you've read about giants to explain your answer.

PLAN First, write or draw one thing you *should* do in the "Do" box. Next, write or draw one thing you *should not* do in the "Don't" box.

Do	Don't

WRITE Now write a list of tips to help someone make friends with a giant. Remember to:

- Include tips that tell what to do and what *not* to do.

- Use what you know about giants from *Jack and the Beanstalk* and other stories you have read.

_____

_____

_____

_____

_____

_____

_____

_____

_____

_____

Prepare to Read

GENRE STUDY **Fairy tales** are old stories that have made-up characters and events that could not happen. As you read *Jackie and the Beanstalk,* look for:

- clues that the story is make-believe
- an ending that is happy
- how pictures and words help you understand what happens

SET A PURPOSE As you read, **make connections** by finding ways that this text is like things in your life and other texts you have read. This will help you understand and remember the text.

POWER WORDS

adorable

oversized

hauling

glanced

Meet Lori Mortensen.

JACKIE
AND THE
BEANSTALK

by Lori Mortensen

illustrated by Ben Scruton

Once upon a time, a girl named Jackie lived in an apartment with her father.

It was crowded and messy because they lived with a GIGANTIC cow.

What was a cow doing there? Eating, mostly.

It eats like a cow!

Buying the cow had been a stupendously bad idea, but nobody thought of that when it was a cute little calf.

Adorable! Can we buy it?

Sure!

But nobody wanted a cow—not firefighters, not florists, not taxi drivers.
42
42
42
12 8TH ST FLORIST
OPEN
TAXI
Just when Jackie was about to give up, a mysterious woman walked up to her.
How much for the oversized moo-er?
DINER
417
One hundred dollars!

The woman had no money, but she did have some special beans.

Plant them in some dirt, add some water, and wait. By morning, SHAZAM! There'll be a beanstalk stretching up to the sky like a winding green staircase.

Are you sure? Plant growth takes dirt, water, sun, and time!

Jackie looked at the cow and then looked at the beans. Suddenly, pocketing the beans sounded a whole lot better than hauling the cow back home.

Deal!

Of course, when Jackie got home, her father hit the roof. Well, not really, but he did toss the beans out the window and yell a lot.

Overnight, the beans sprouted long, green tendrils that twisted and reached up toward the sky.

A few beans for a whole cow?

The next morning, there it was, exactly as the woman promised—the biggest beanstalk Jackie had ever seen.

Wow! I've never seen a plant grow so fast! I wonder what's at the top. Maybe there's treasure!

Did Jackie ever find treasure? No, but she did start a business that turned into a gigantic success . . .

. . . and lived happily ever after.

Turn and Talk

Use details from *Jackie and the Beanstalk* to answer these questions with a partner.

1. **Make Connections** How are *Jackie and the Beanstalk* and *Jack and the Beanstalk* alike? How are they different?

2. Why do you think Jackie's father lets her get a cow for a pet? What causes him to change his mind about it?

3. What problem does Jackie have after she climbs the beanstalk? How does she solve it?

Talking Tip

Share your ideas. Speak clearly and not too fast or too slow.

I think that _____.

Write a Story

PROMPT How would the story be different if the cow told it? Think about how the cow's point of view is different from the other characters'. Use details from the words and pictures to explain your ideas.

PLAN First, draw or write what happens first, next, and last in the cow's story.

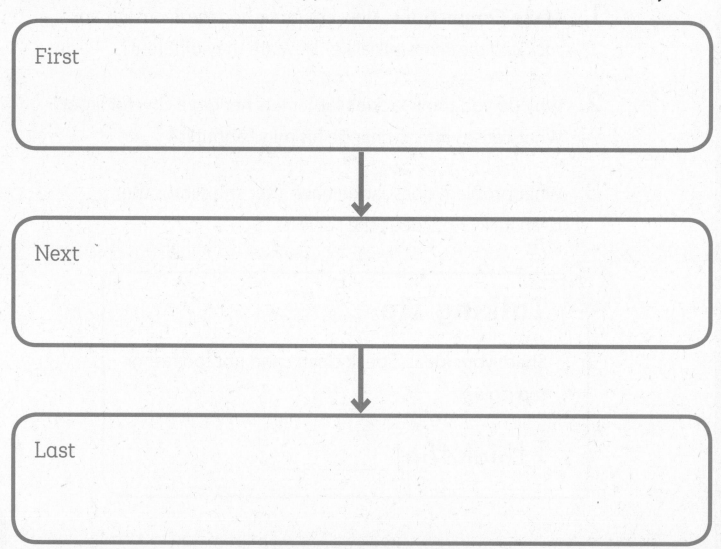

First

Next

Last

WRITE Now write the cow's version of the story. Help your readers get to know the cow! Include details that tell what she is like and how she feels about the story events. Remember to:

- Tell the story events in order.

- Use the words *I* and *me* to write in the cow's voice.

_____

_____

_____

_____

_____

_____

_____

_____

_____

_____

Prepare to Read

GENRE STUDY **Informational text** is nonfiction. It gives facts about a topic. As you read *Don't Touch Me!,* look for:

- captions with photos

- details and facts about a topic

- how visuals and words help you understand the text

SET A PURPOSE Read to find out the most important ideas in each part. Then **synthesize,** or put together these ideas in your mind, to find out what the text really means to you.

POWER WORDS

sharp

prickles

thorns

extra

poke

nasty

sensitive

attack

Build Background: Plant Predators

DON'T TOUCH ME!

by
Elizabeth Preston

Plants can't run away from hungry animals. So some of them fight back. They have defenses to keep creatures from eating them. These plants can scratch you or stab you. Some of them can make you sick. Others make you itch like crazy. Don't get too close, or you'll be sorry!

146

OW

Do you have a rose bush in your yard? Then you know these pretty flowers are better for sniffing than touching. Roses have sharp prickles on their stems. Some other plants, like the hawthorn, have woody thorns.

And beautiful holly leaves have very sharp points. (Holly leaves and berries have extra protection. They're poisonous!)

147

Cactus plants keep animals away with spines. Some cacti have arms—but hugging them is a bad idea.

OW OW OW OW

Yowch!

A stinging nettle doesn't look as dangerous as a spiny cactus. But it's covered with sharp hairs called trichomes. The hairs are like tiny needles. If you touch them, they poke your skin with chemicals that sting and itch. You might get a nasty rash.

Itch

Poison ivy leaves have oils that can make you itchy. If your soccer ball rolls into a patch of poison ivy during a game, you might be scratching later. Poison oak and poison smac are related plants that make the same oils. You can watch out for poison ivy by remembering the rhyme, "Leaves of three, let it be!"

Shy Plants

The sensitive or touch-me-not plant doesn't stab you, poison you, or make you itch. If you touch it, the plant quickly folds up its leaves.

Plants with Ants

Acacia trees have big, scary thorns. But for extra protection, they use ants. The ants have a special friendship with the tree. They live inside hollow thorns and eat food the tree makes for them. If a bug or a bigger animal comes too close, the ants attack and sting it.

Use details from *Don't Touch Me!* to answer these questions with a partner.

1. **Synthesize** How do plants protect themselves?

2. Why did the author write this text? What is she trying to persuade readers to do?

3. Compare and contrast *Don't Touch Me!* and *Experiment with What a Plant Needs to Grow*. How are the texts alike? What are the most important differences between them?

Talking Tip

Say your ideas. Speak clearly and not too fast or too slow.

I think that _____.

Write an Opinion

PROMPT In your opinion, which plant in *Don't Touch Me!* has the most extreme defenses? Look for details in the words and pictures to help you decide.

PLAN First, write which plant you chose in the chart. Then write or draw reasons why you chose that plant.

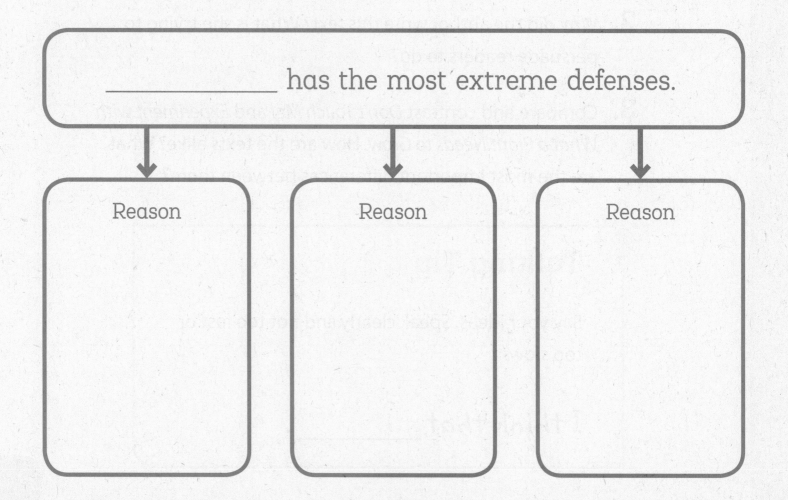

_____ has the most extreme defenses.

| Reason | Reason | Reason |

WRITE Now write your opinion about the plant you chose. Include reasons why you think that plant's defenses are the most extreme. Remember to:

- Use details from the words and photos.

- Use describing words.

_____

_____

_____

_____

_____

_____

_____

_____

_____

Prepare to View

GENRE STUDY ▶ **Videos** are short movies that give you information or something for you to watch for enjoyment. As you watch *George Washington Carver: The Wizard of Tuskegee,* look for:

- how pictures, sounds, and words work together
- information about the topic
- the purpose of the video

SET A PURPOSE ▶ Ask yourself what happens and why to find **cause and effect** connections in the video. A cause is something that makes something else happen. An effect is what happens because of the cause.

Build Background: Made from Peanuts

As You View Get to know George Washington Carver! Think about how puppets, rhyming words, and sound effects help to tell Mr. Carver's story in a fun way. Listen for details that tell what happened and why to help you understand how the events in his life are connected.

Use details from *George Washington Carver: The Wizard of Tuskegee* to answer these questions with a partner.

1. **Cause and Effect** What caused George Washington Carver to move to Tuskegee? What effect did that have on his work?

2. What did George do when he wasn't allowed to go to his neighborhood school? What does that tell you about him?

3. What does the narrator mean when he says that George "reached for the sky"?

Talking Tip

Add your own idea to your partner's. Be polite.

I like your idea. My idea
is _____.

Let's Wrap Up!

(?) Essential Question

What do plants need to live and grow?

· ·

Pick one of these activities to show what you have learned about the topic.

1. Plant Instructions

You have read about what a plant needs to grow. Now, write instructions that tell someone how to grow a healthy plant. List the things he or she will need and the steps to follow. Draw pictures to go with each step in your instructions.

Word Challenge

Can you use the word survive in your instructions?

2. Grow a Poem

Work with a partner to write a poem about plants. Take turns writing one line for the poem and watch your poem grow. Be sure to include details you learned from the texts.

My Notes

Home Sweet Habitat

"What is not good for the hive
is not good for the bee."

—Latin Proverb

How do living things in a habitat depend on each other?

Get Curious

Video

Words About Animal Habitats

Complete the Vocabulary Network to show what you know about the words.

ecosystem

Meaning: An **ecosystem** is all the animals and plants that live in the same area.

Synonyms and Antonyms	Drawing

habitat

Meaning: A **habitat** is a place where plants and animals live and grow.

Synonyms and Antonyms	Drawing

species

Meaning: A **species** is a group of animals or plants that are alike.

Synonyms and Antonyms	Drawing

The Best Habitat for Me

An animal's habitat is the place where it lives. I'm a red panda, and my habitat is a cool, dark forest. In my opinion, it is the finest habitat in the world! The forest ecosystem has everything I need, so it is the best place for me to live.

A good habitat, like mine, should provide shelter. The forest has lots of trees. That is where I spend most of my time. The trees provide a place for me to sleep, especially during the hottest part of the day. Trees also keep me safe. The color of my fur helps me blend in with the trees so other animals can't see me as well. I can climb tall trees to escape if I am being chased.

A good habitat should also provide food. Mostly, I eat bamboo. Many different species of bamboo grow in my habitat. I like to eat the shoots and leaves. Some of my other favorite foods are fruit, roots, and acorns. The insects I find on the ground are tasty, too.

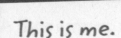

This is me.

ZZ ZZZ

Here I am taking a nap.

Bamboo leaves are yummy!

All animals need food and shelter. Some animals find these things in other habitats, like deserts or prairies. I have everything I need right here in the forest. Nothing is nicer than waking up in my favorite tree and knowing a tasty meal is close by. My forest home is the perfect home for me!

Home Sweet Home

It can be hard to see me in the trees.

Prepare to Read

GENRE STUDY **Informational text** is nonfiction. It gives facts about a topic. As you read *The Long, Long Journey*, pay attention to:

- order of events
- main topic and details
- how pictures and words help you understand the text

SET A PURPOSE **Ask questions** before, during, and after you read to help you get information or understand the text. Look for evidence in the text and pictures to **answer** your questions.

POWER WORDS

wobbly
trills
crouches
coast
prances
flock
route
mingles

Meet Sandra Markle.

THE LONG, LONG JOURNEY

BY SANDRA MARKLE

ILLUSTRATED BY MIA POSADA

Crackle!
Crackle!
Crunch!

The little female bar–tailed godwit at last breaks free of her egg. She steps into the world on long, wobbly legs. It's nearly midnight, but it's June in Alaska and still light. A cool wind blows the chick's downy coat. She shivers, lifts her beak, and squeaks, "Peep! Peep!"

The little female was the last to hatch. Two sisters and a brother are nearby, with their father. They are hunting insects in the grass. Their mother next to the nest trills softly, and the chicks come running.

They huddle with their sister, and their mother settles over them. This way, the newest chick stays warm and joins the family.

For two days, the chicks stay close to the nest. Their parents take turns sitting on them to keep them warm. In between these rests, parents and chicks search for food. The parents need to double their body weight before fall. The chicks need to grow up and become strong.

The little female learns to hunt spiders, crane fly larvae, and beetles. She eats all she can find.

Soon the little godwit and her family wander farther as they feed. But they are rarely alone. Lots of other godwits nest and feed in this treeless land. Sometimes other hunters come searching for food too.

One day, an Arctic fox sneaks up and slips close to the little female.

But her father spots the fox and squawks a warning.

The little female is not yet able to fly. She crouches low and stays still. Her coloring helps her blend in with the grass. Her father flaps his wings and swoops at the fox.

Her mother joins the attack and so do other adult godwits. The fox runs off without its meal.

For almost a month, the female godwit chick eats and eats and grows bigger. She also grows feathers and loses her fluffy down coat.

When the chick isn't eating, she's hopping and flapping her wings. Her wings grow stronger with each hop-flap.

Then one day, the young female godwit hops and flaps hard. For the first time, she does what godwits do best.

She flies.

174

In mid-August, the mother godwit leaves. The young birds stay near their father. They eat and practice flying hour after hour so their wings grow even stronger. At last, they follow their father to the coast. They join thousands of godwits gathered on Alaska's Cape Avinof mudflats.

The young female prances across the mud on her long legs. Every step or two, she pokes her long beak deep into the muddy ground to find and eat tunneling worms and tiny clams.

In September, flock after flock of adult godwits leave the mudflats.

By mid-October, mostly only young birds remain. The young female is one of the flock. She practices flying with the other godwits. In between flights, she feeds alongside them. She eats and eats, growing very plump.

Finally, when dark clouds sweep overhead, the young female rises with the flock. She is pushed southward by strong winds. Her long journey has begun.

The young female flies through unfamiliar skies and over unknown seas.

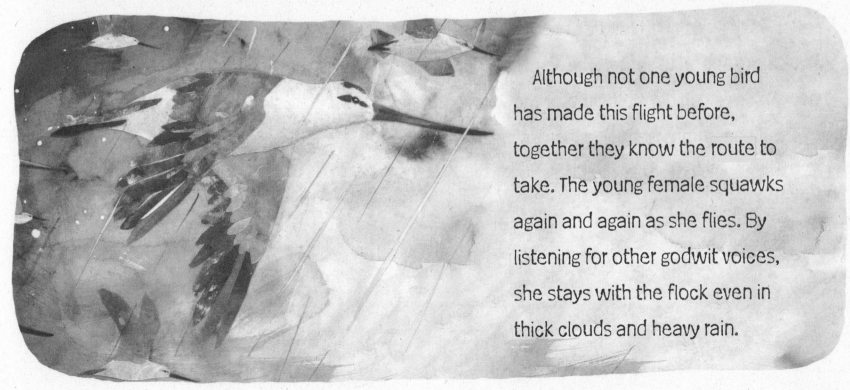

Although not one young bird has made this flight before, together they know the route to take. The young female squawks again and again as she flies. By listening for other godwit voices, she stays with the flock even in thick clouds and heavy rain.

One day, a peregrine falcon hunting over an island swoops out of the clouds with wings folded and talon-tipped toes stretched out.

The falcon aims straight for the young female, but she pumps her wings hard, climbs fast, and escapes! Another godwit isn't so lucky.

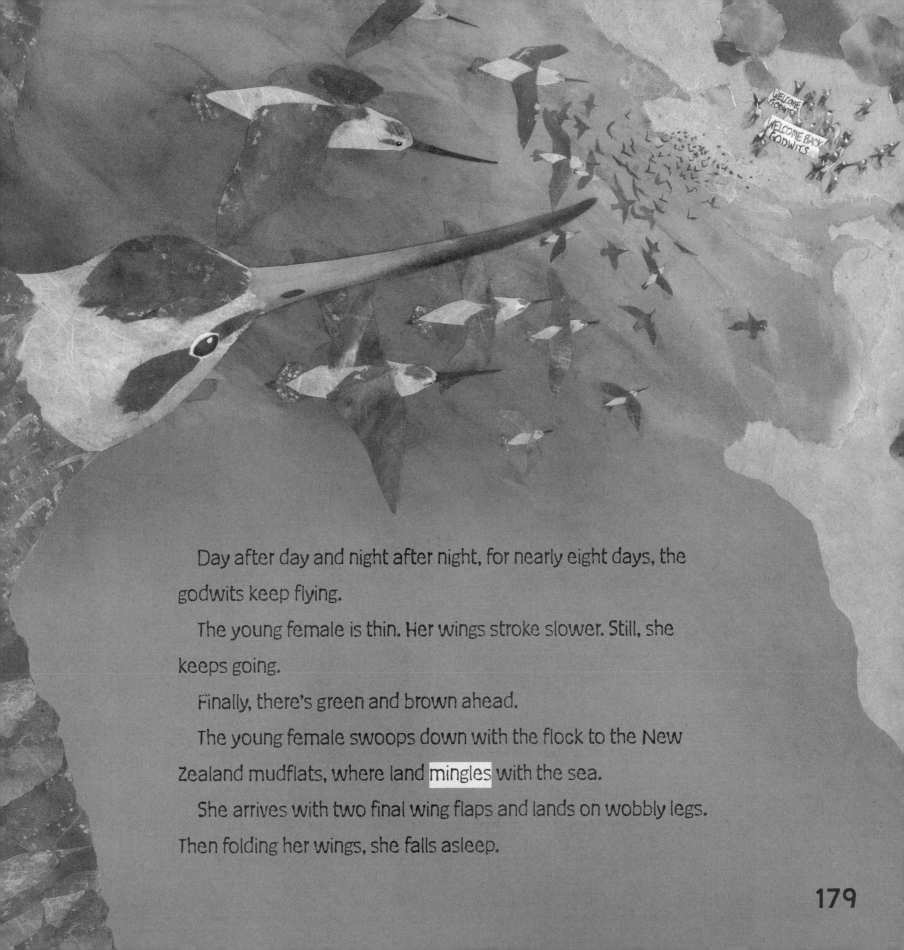

Day after day and night after night, for nearly eight days, the godwits keep flying.

The young female is thin. Her wings stroke slower. Still, she keeps going.

Finally, there's green and brown ahead.

The young female swoops down with the flock to the New Zealand mudflats, where land mingles with the sea.

She arrives with two final wing flaps and lands on wobbly legs. Then folding her wings, she falls asleep.

179

The young female doesn't sleep for long, though. She needs to eat to get back her strength. She'll stay in New Zealand for two years until she's ready to raise a family of her own. Then, when March brings cool winds, she'll once again join the godwit flock and make the long, long journey back to Alaska.

Turn and Talk

Use details from *The Long, Long Journey* to answer these questions with a partner.

1. **Ask and Answer Questions** What questions did you ask yourself about the godwit before, during, and after reading? How did your questions help you understand the text?

2. Godwit chicks stay with their parents when they are young. How does this help them survive?

3. Using what you learned from the text, explain what it would be like to be a godwit chick.

Talking Tip

Listen carefully and politely. Say what you like about your partner's ideas.

Write a Travel Journal

PROMPT How would the young godwit describe her migration from Alaska to New Zealand? What does she see, hear, and feel? Use details from the text and illustrations to explain your ideas.

PLAN First, find details in the words and illustrations that show what the godwit sees, hears, and feels during her long journey. Add them to the chart.

Sees	Hears	Feels

WRITE Now write a travel journal entry from the godwit's point of view that tells about her journey. Remember to:

- Use the words *I* and *me* to describe the journey the way the godwit would.

- Describe the events of her journey in order.

_____

_____

_____

_____

_____

_____

_____

_____

_____

_____

Prepare to Read

GENRE STUDY **Informational text** is nonfiction. It gives facts about a topic. As you read *Sea Otter Pups,* pay attention to:

- details and facts about a topic
- maps that help explain a topic
- pictures with labels

SET A PURPOSE As you read, stop and think if you don't understand something. Reread, ask yourself questions, use what you already know, and look for visual clues to help you understand the text.

POWER WORDS

surface

wraps

attached

crack

Build Background: Ocean Habitat

Sea Otter Pups

by Ruth Owen

Meet a sea otter pup

A mother sea otter and her pup are floating in the ocean. The mother otter is resting on her back. The little pup is cuddled up on his mother's belly, just above the water.

mother sea otter

sea otter pup

What is a sea otter?

Sea otters are animals that live in the ocean. They are about as big as a medium-size dog. Sea otters have very thick fur. The fur helps keep the otter's body warm and dry in the cold water.

Adult sea otter size

adult sea otter

thick fur

Where do sea otters live?

Although sea otters live in the ocean, they stay close to the shore. The yellow parts of this map show where sea otters live.

shore

sea otters

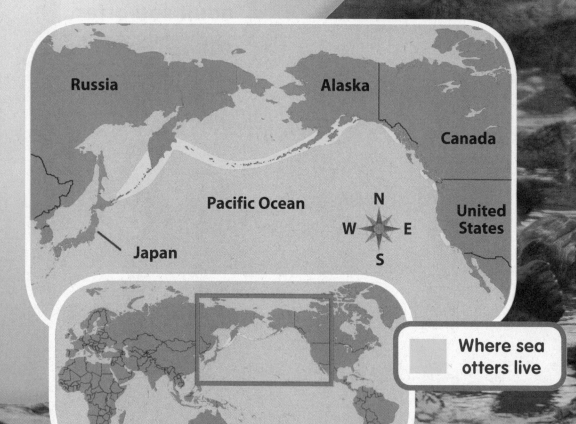

Russia

Alaska

Canada

Pacific Ocean

United States

Japan

N
W E
S

Where sea otters live

mother sea otter

one-week-old pup

A newborn pup

A mother sea otter gives birth in the ocean to just one pup at a time. After the pup is born, she places it on her chest to keep it warm. Then she feeds it milk from her body. A pup drinks its mother's milk until it's about four to six months old.

Learning to swim

A newborn sea otter cannot swim, but it can float really well. It floats on top of the water like a beach ball! The mother sea otter gives her pup swimming lessons. By the time it is about 14 weeks old, the pup is able to swim and dive.

floating mother sea otter

floating pup

Sea otter food

Sea otter adults and pups eat crabs, clams, and other shellfish. The mother otter dives under the water to hunt for food. She teaches the pup how to dive and find shellfish, too.

clam

mother otter

crab

pup

Time for dinner

Once the mother sea otter finds a clam, she swims back up to the water's surface. She also brings a rock with her and lays it on her belly. Then she smashes the clam onto the rock to open its shell. The mother otter and the pup share the clam meat.

clam

sea otter pup

mother otter

clam meat

sleeping adult
sea otter

kelp

Goodnight!

When it is time to sleep, an adult sea otter sometimes wraps seaweed around its body. The seaweed, called kelp, is attached to the ocean floor. It holds the otter in one place. This keeps the waves from carrying the otter out into the ocean. Sometimes the mother otter also wraps kelp around the pup as it sleeps on her chest.

193

Growing up

When a pup is between 6 and 12 months old, it leaves its mother. It knows how to dive underwater to hunt for food. It can use rocks to crack open shellfish. The pup is now ready to begin its grown-up life!

clam meat

clams

194

Turn and Talk

Use details from *Sea Otter Pups* to answer these questions with a partner.

1. **Monitor and Clarify** What did you do when you came to a part of the text that you didn't understand? Tell how it helped or didn't help you.

2. Which details in the text help you figure out the topic and central idea?

3. Compare the animal habitats in *Sea Otter Pups* and *The Long, Long Journey*. How do the habitats meet the animals' needs?

Talking Tip

Answer your partner's questions. Explain your ideas clearly.

I mean that _____.

Write a Description

PROMPT Imagine that you are a scientist observing a mother sea otter and her pup in their habitat. Describe what you see and hear. Use details from the text and photographs to help you.

PLAN First, make notes about what the habitat is like. Next, make notes about the sea otters. What do they look like? What are they doing?

Habitat	Sea Otters

Sea Otter Pups
by Ruth Owen

WRITE Now write a description of a mother sea otter and her pup in their habitat. Remember to:

- Use exact adjectives to describe the otters and their habitat.

- Include details that show how the habitat helps them survive.

_____

_____

_____

_____

_____

_____

_____

_____

_____

_____

Prepare to Read

GENRE STUDY **Poetry** uses images, sounds, and rhythm to express feelings. As you read the poems in *At Home in the Wild*, pay attention to:

- repetition of words or lines
- words that describe
- rhythm, or beats, between words

SET A PURPOSE As you read, **create mental images,** or make pictures in your mind, to help you understand details in the text.

POWER WORDS

sheltered
....
weary
....
hide
....
wit

Build Background: Animal Homes

At Home
in the Wild

Poetry and Song

Polar Bear Family

by Eileen Spinelli

Polar bear mama moves with grace
to find a sheltered winter place.
She digs a snow cave wide and deep
where she and baby cubs can sleep.

Come spring, the cubs set out for fun.
They romp all day in the Arctic sun.
They slip and slide. They race and roam.
Then, weary, ride their mama home.

201

Big Brown Moose

by Joyce Sidman

I'm a big brown moose,

I'm a rascally moose,

I'm a moose with a tough, shaggy hide;

and I kick and I prance

in a long-legged dance

with my moose-mama close by my side.

I shrug off the cold

and I sneeze at the wind

and I swivel my ears in the snow;

and I tramp and I tromp

over forest and swamp,

'cause there's nowhere a moose cannot go.

I'm a big brown moose,

I'm a ravenous moose

as I hunt for the willow and yew;

with a snort and a crunch,

I rip off each bunch,

and I chew and I chew and I chew.

202

When together we slump
in a comfortable clump—
my mountainous mama and I—
I give her a nuzzle
of velvety muzzle.
Our frosty breath drifts to the sky.

I'm a big brown moose,
I'm a slumberous moose,
I'm a moose with a warm, snuggly hide;
and I bask in the moon
as the coyotes croon,
with my moose-mama close by my side.

203

Over in the Meadow

1. O-ver in the mea-dow, in the sand, in the sun,

Lived a sweet moth-er frog and her lit-tle frog-gie one.

"Croak!" said the mo-ther; "I croak," said the one, So

they croaked and they croaked in the sand, in the sun.

2. Over in the meadow, in the stream so blue,
   Lived a shiny mother fish and her little fishies two.
   "Swim!" said the mother; "We swim," said the two,
   So they swam and they swam in the stream so blue.

3. Over in the meadow, on a branch of the tree,
   Lived a wise mother bird and her little birdies three.
   "Sing!" said the mother; "We sing," said the three,
   So they sang and they sang on a branch of the tree.

4. Over in the meadow, at a den near the shore,
   Lived a mighty mother wolf and her little cubs four.
   "Howl!" said the mother; "We howl," said the four,
   So they howled and they howled at their den near the shore.

5. Over in the meadow, in a busy beehive,
   Lived a fuzzy mother bee and her little bees five.
   "Buzz!" said the mother; "We buzz," said the five,
   So they buzzed and they buzzed in a busy beehive.

206

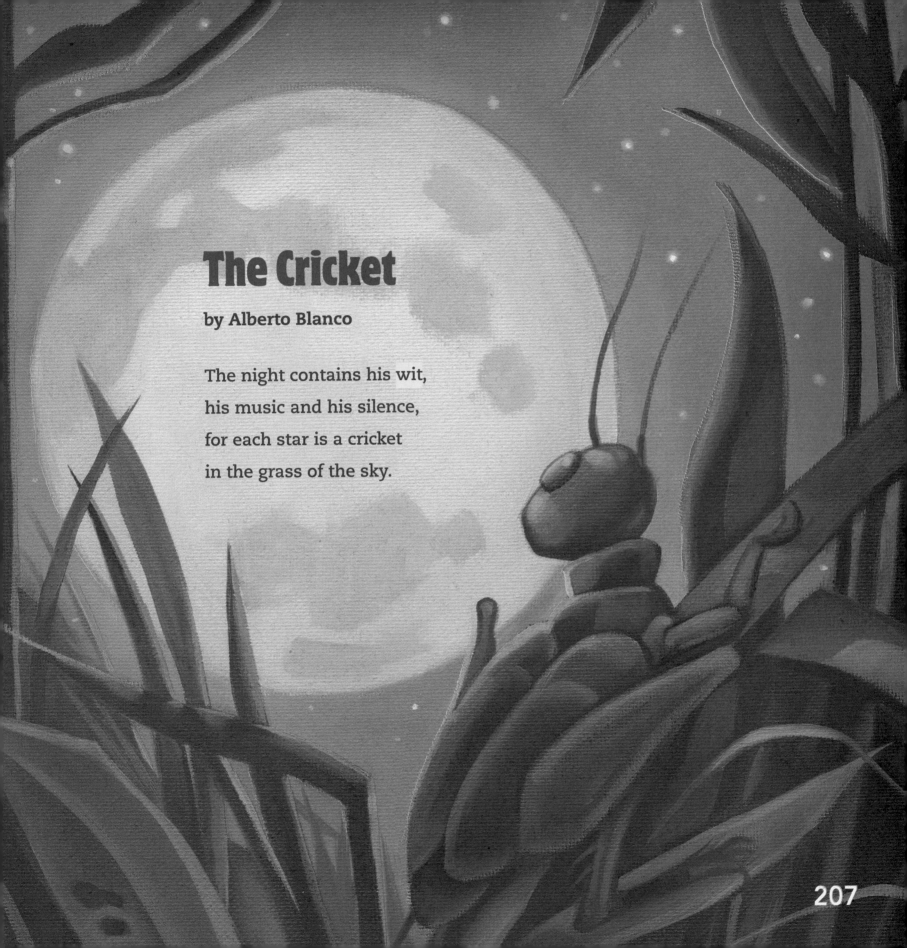

The Cricket

by Alberto Blanco

The night contains his wit,
his music and his silence,
for each star is a cricket
in the grass of the sky.

The Ant

by Alma Flor Ada
and F. Isabel Campoy

Here comes the ant
Out of its hole,
Grabs a grain of wheat
And returns like a mole.

Another ant comes
Out of its hole,
Grabs a grain of wheat
And returns like a mole.

ANOTHER ant comes
Out of its hole . . .

Turn and Talk

Use details from *At Home in the Wild* to answer these questions with a partner.

1. **Create Mental Images** Close your eyes. Picture walking in a habitat in one of the poems. What would you see, hear, and feel? Which of the poet's words help you create the picture?

2. If "The Ant" were longer, what would the next line be? Why do you think the poet uses repetition in this poem?

3. How do the poems make you feel? How do the poets use rhythm and rhyme to create those feelings?

Talking Tip

Ask to learn more about your partner's ideas.

Please explain _____.

Write a Song

PROMPT How could you change "Over in the Meadow" to make it about a different animal habitat? Look carefully at the song. Notice the rhyme pattern and repetition. Which words would you need to change to describe another habitat?

PLAN First, choose the habitat you will write about. On one side of the chart, list animals that live there. On the other side, list the sounds the animals make.

Animals	Animal Sounds

WRITE Now change the words in "Over in the Meadow" to write your own animal habitats song! Remember to:

- Include details that tell what the animal habitat is like.

- Use words that fit the rhyming pattern of the song.

_____

_____

_____

_____

_____

_____

_____

_____

_____

_____

Prepare to Read

GENRE STUDY   **Folktales** are old tales passed down over time through storytelling. When you read *Abuelo and the Three Bears,* look for:

- animal characters that act and talk like people
- author's purpose (to entertain or explain?)
- the beginning, middle, and ending of the story
- how pictures and words help you understand what happens

SET A PURPOSE   As you read, **retell** the story. Use your own words to tell what happened in the beginning, middle, and end of the story.

POWER WORDS

arrive

grumpy

joking

tucked

stubborn

growled

shrugged

offered

Build Background: Bears

ABUELO AND THE THREE BEARS

by Jerry Tello

illustrated by Ana López Escrivá

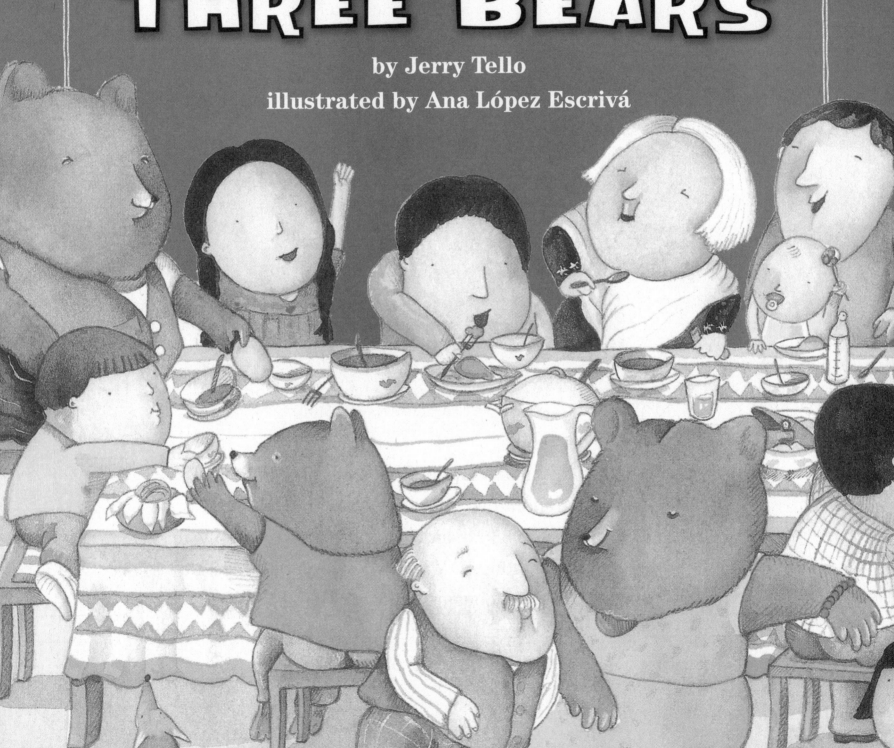

It was a quiet Sunday. Emilio and his grandfather sat on the front porch.

"Abuelo," said Emilio, "do we have to wait much longer? When will everybody get here?"

"Your cousins will arrive soon," Abuelo answered, "and we'll have a fine dinner. I'll tell you a story to help pass the time."

Once there were three bears who lived in the woods—
Papá Bear, Mamá Bear, and their little Osito. One Sunday
morning, Papá Bear woke up as grumpy as ever. Then he
smelled something good. "Mmmm, frijoles!" he said.

"Abuelo, you're joking!" laughed Emilio.
"Bears don't like beans!"
"Well, all the bears I know like frijoles,"
said Abuelo.

Papá Bear got up and rushed down to the kitchen.

"Buenos días," said Papá Bear to Mamá Bear and Osito.

Papá Bear sat down at the table and tucked a napkin under his chin. "How are the frijoles? Are they ready yet?" he asked. "Yes," answered Mamá Bear, "but they're still too hot to eat."

"I can't wait," said Papá Bear. "I'm so hungry I could eat an elephant."

"Abuelo," said Emilio, "bears don't eat elephants."

"Emilio," answered Abuelo, "you must never argue with a hungry bear."

217

Stubborn Papá Bear didn't listen to Mamá Bear's warning.

"¡Ay!" he growled, jumping out of his chair. "These beans are too hot!"

"I told you so," said Mamá Bear. "Why don't we take a walk into town while they cool?"

"All right," grumbled Papá Bear, whose mouth was still burning. So the bears left their breakfast to cool and went out.

Just then, in another part of the woods, a girl named Trencitas set out from her house to visit her friend, Osito. She was called Trencitas because she had long black braids.

"Abuelo," Emilio called out, "the girl in this story is called Goldilocks and she has blond hair."

"Goldilocks?" Abuelo shrugged. "In my story it was Trencitas with her long black braids who came to visit. And she was hungry, too!"

When Trencitas arrived at Osito's house, she noticed that the door was open. So she stepped inside and followed her nose until she came to the three bowls of beans.

First Trencitas tasted some beans from the great big bowl, but they were too hot. Then she tasted some from the medium-sized bowl, but they were too cold. Finally she tasted some from the little bowl, and they were just right. So she finished them all up.

Now Trencitas decided to sit in the living room and wait for the bears to return. She sat in the great big chair, but it was too hard. She sat in the medium-sized chair, but it was too soft. Then she sat in the little chair, and it was just right until . . . CRASH!

"Abuelo, what's Trencitas going to do?" asked Emilio. "She broke her friend's chair."

"Don't worry," Abuelo said. "She'll come back later with glue and leave it like new."

Trencitas was feeling very sleepy. She went upstairs to take a rest. First she tried the great big bed, but the blanket was scratchy. Then she tried the medium-sized bed, but it was too lumpy. Finally she tried the little bed. It was too small, but it was so cozy and soft that Trencitas soon fell asleep.

When the three bears came home, Papá Bear headed straight to the kitchen to eat his frijoles.

"¡Ay!" he growled when he saw his bowl. "Somebody's been eating my beans."

"And somebody's been eating my beans," said Mamá Bear.

"And there's only one bean left in my bowl," said Osito.

Then the three bears went into the living room.

"¡Ay!" said Papá Bear, when he saw that his chair had been moved. "Somebody's been sitting in my chair."

"And somebody's been sitting in my chair," said Mamá Bear.

"And my chair is all over the place!" said Osito.

The three bears climbed the stairs to check out the bedrooms. Papá Bear went first. Mamá Bear and Osito followed behind him.

"¡Ay!" said Papá Bear, when he looked in the bedroom. "Somebody's been sleeping in my bed."

"And somebody's been sleeping in my bed," said Mamá Bear.

"Look who's sleeping in my bed!" said Osito. He ran over to Trencitas and woke her up. Then they all had a good laugh.

By now it was getting late. Mamá Bear said they'd walk Trencitas home to make sure she got there safely.

Papá Bear did not like this idea. "Another walk!" he growled. "What about my frijoles?"

"There'll be beans at my house," offered Trencitas.

"I'll bet that made Papá Bear happy," said Emilio.

"You're right," said Abuelo. "Here's what happened next . . . ."

When they all arrived at Trencitas's house, they sat down at a long table with Trencitas's parents, grandparents, uncles, aunts, and lots of cousins. They ate pork and fish and chicken and tortillas and beans and salsa so hot it brought tears to their eyes. And they laughed and shared stories.

"So you see, Emilio," said Abuelo, "Papá Bear had to wait a long time to eat his frijoles. But, in the end, he had a wonderful meal and lots of fun, just as you will when your cousins arrive."

"Is that the end of the story?" Emilio asked.

"Yes," answered Abuelo, "and it's the end of your waiting, too!"

GLOSSARY

Abuelo	Grandfather
Osito	Little Bear
Frijoles	Beans
Buenos días	Good morning
¡Ay!	Oh!
Trencitas	Little Braids
Tortillas	Thin corn pancakes
Salsa	Spicy tomato and chile dip

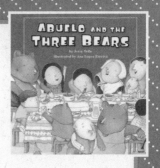

Use details from *Abuelo and the Three Bears* to answer these questions with a partner.

1. **Retell** Take turns telling the story events in order. Use order words such as *first, next, after,* and *at the end* to help you.

2. Who is telling the story? How would the story be different if one of the three bears were telling it?

3. How is this story like another story you know? How is it different? Compare the characters, setting, and events in both stories.

Talking Tip

Be polite. Wait for your turn to talk. Then tell your idea to your partner.

I think that _____.

Cite Text Evidence

Write a Drama

PROMPT Imagine you wake up at the three bears' house. What happens next? Write a short drama to tell what happens. Look back at the text and illustrations for ideas.

PLAN First, draw or write what will happen first, next, and last in your drama.

First

Next

Last

WRITE Now write your drama. Include details in the dialogue that bring your characters to life. Remember to:

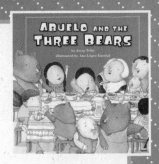

- Name the **characters** and the **setting.**

- Include **stage directions** to show what the characters are feeling or doing.

- Include a **narrator** to help describe the action.

_____

_____

_____

_____

_____

_____

_____

_____

_____

Prepare to View

GENRE STUDY **Videos** are short movies that give you information or something for you to watch for enjoyment. As you watch *Ducklings Jump from Nest,* notice:

- how pictures, sounds, and words work together
- what the video is about
- information about the topic
- the tone or mood of the video

SET A PURPOSE One way that events can be told is in **chronological order.** That means they are told in the order they happened. Pay attention to the order of events in the video. How does the order help you understand how the events are related?

Build Background: Nests

DUCKLINGS JUMP
FROM NEST

by Terra Mater Factual Studios

As You View These little ducklings are about to have a big adventure! As you watch, think about the order of events in the video. Pay attention to how the visuals, words, and sounds help you understand what it is like to be inside the ducklings' nest.

Use details from *Ducklings Jump from Nest* to answer these questions with a partner.

1. **Chronological Order** What do the ducklings do while their mom is in the nest? What do they do after she jumps out of the nest?

2. What does the narrator mean when he says, "some ducklings aren't as bold as others"?

3. How does the video make you feel? How do the narrator's words and the music help to make you feel that way?

Listening Tip

Listen carefully. Think about the meaning of what your partner says.

Let's Wrap Up!

(?) **Essential Question**

How do living things in a habitat depend on each other?

....

Pick one of these activities to show what you have learned about the topic.

1. Imagine That! Story

Choose an animal habitat you read about. Imagine that the whole world is made up of that habitat. How would it change the way some animals and people live? Write a story that tells what it would be like. Include details you learned from the texts.

2. Habitat Trivia

Work with a partner. Write three questions about the habitats you read about. Be sure that the answers are in one of the texts you read. Then, play habitat trivia in a group. Challenge each other to answer your habitat questions.

Word Challenge

Can you use the word species in one of your questions?

My Notes

Many Cultures, One World

"We are all the same and we are all different.
What great friends we will be."

—Kelly Moran

What can we learn from different people and cultures?

Get Curious
Video

Words About World Cultures

Complete the Vocabulary Network to show what you know about the words.

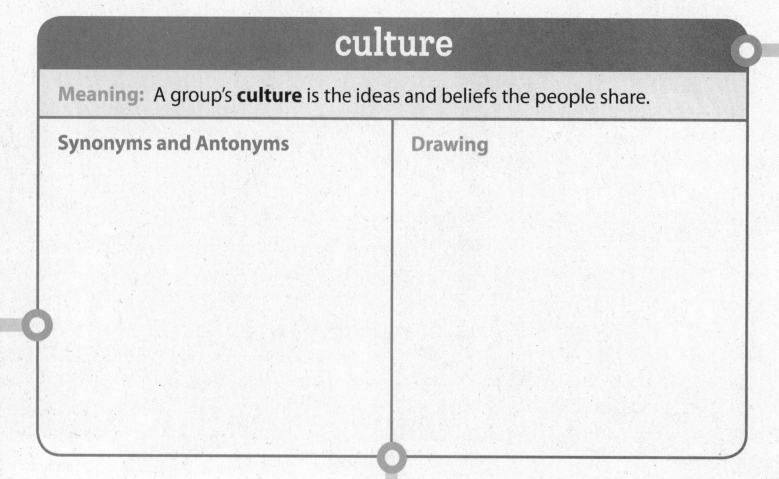

culture

Meaning: A group's **culture** is the ideas and beliefs the people share.

Synonyms and Antonyms	Drawing

harmony

Meaning: Being in **harmony** means living together in a peaceful way.

Synonyms and Antonyms	Drawing

heritage

Meaning: A country's **heritage** is its way of doing things that is passed down over time.

Synonyms and Antonyms	Drawing

Hello, World!

If you took a trip around the world, you would learn about different cultures and traditions. You would meet different people, taste different foods, and hear different kinds of music. You would also hear different languages.

Germany

China

Kenya

Argentina

Every country has special ways of saying *hello*, *goodbye*, and *thank you*.

Understanding different languages and traditions helps us live in harmony. What traditions are part of your heritage?

Argentina

hello = hola (OH-lah)
goodbye = chau (CHOW)
thank you = gracias (GRAH-see-us)

China

hello = nǐ hǎo (nee-HOW)
goodbye = zài jiàn (ZYE-chin)
thank you = xiè xiè (SYEH-syeh)

Kenya

hello = jambo (JAHM-boh)
goodbye = kwaheri (kwah-HEH-ree)
thank you = asante (uh-SAHN-tay)

Germany

hello = hallo (HAH-low)
goodbye = auf wiedersehen
(OWF VEE-dur-zayn)
thank you = danke (DAHN-kuh)

243

Prepare to Read

GENRE STUDY **Realistic fiction** stories are made up but could happen in real life. When you read *Where on Earth Is My Bagel?*, look for:

- characters that act and talk like real people
- problems and solutions
- ways pictures and words help readers understand the story

SET A PURPOSE Read to make smart guesses, or **inferences,** about things the author does not say. Use clues in the text and pictures to help you.

POWER WORDS

darting

smothered

nod

slippery

hollered

delight

fragrant

grunted

Meet Grace Lin.

Where on Earth Is My Bagel?

by Frances Park and
Ginger Park

illustrated by Grace Lin

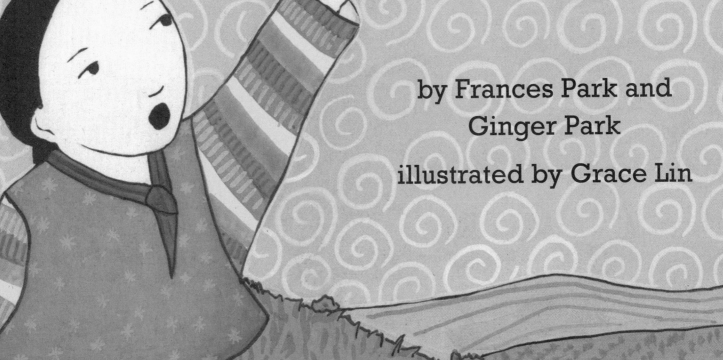

Once there was a boy named Yum Yung who lived in a village where the mountains met the sky. There were waterfalls rushing into streams of darting fish. There were lilacs gently blossoming on every hillside.
But there were no New York bagels!

How a New York bagel popped into Yum Yung's head was a mystery. Perhaps it came to him in a dream, smothered with cream cheese. Or maybe he heard sparrows singing of bagel crumbs in Central Park.

However it happened, Yum Yung could not stop thinking about a golden brown bagel with a curious hole in the middle. The very idea made his tummy growl and his mouth water.

Yum Yung declared:

"I want a bagel!"

247

Now dreaming about a New York bagel and actually eating a New York bagel were worlds apart.

Yum Yung wondered, "Where can I find a bagel?" He wondered and wondered, until he came up with an idea. "I will send a message!" he said.

So he sat on a rock and began to write:

Dear New York,
    I would like to order one bagel to go. Please send it to me as soon as possible.
    Respectfully yours,
    Yum Yung in Korea

Yum Yung carried his message to a mountaintop where birds flocked. Soon a pigeon landed on his shoulder. Yum Yung tied his message to the bird's tiny leg and the pigeon flew off into the clouds.

"Pigeon," he cried out, "please return with my bagel!"

Yum Yung waited and waited on the
mountaintop. He waited until the sun dipped
below the mountain. He waited until the sky was
blanketed with stars. But the pigeon did not return
with his New York bagel.

Yum Yung decided that his bagel must be lost. Perhaps
the pigeon dropped his bagel on the wrong mountaintop.
Or maybe it was delivered to the wrong person.

However it happened, Yum Yung would not give up hope.
A search was in order!

Yum Yung declared:

"Where on Earth is my bagel?"

The next morning Yum Yung visited Farmer
Ahn, who was pushing his plow in a field of wheat.

"Excuse me, Farmer Ahn," Yum Yung said.
"Have you seen my missing bagel?"

Farmer Ahn wiped the sweat off his forehead.
"Bagel? What in a farmer's field is a bagel?"

250

"It is round and it has a hole in the middle," Yum Yung explained.

"Hmm," Farmer Ahn said with a nod. He pointed to his plow wheel. "Is that a bagel?"

Yum Yung frowned. "No, that is not my bagel."

"I am sorry, Yum Yung," Farmer Ahn said. "I know about wheat that grows from the rich brown earth, but I know nothing about bagels."

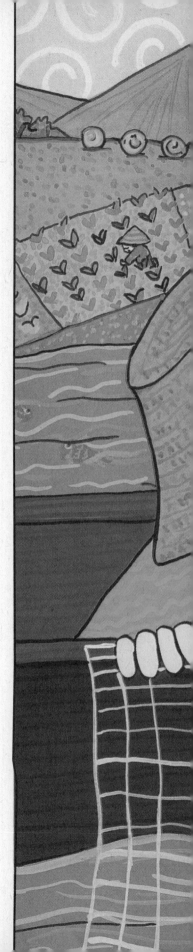

Next Yum Yung visited Fisherman Kee, who was on his boat shaking slippery fish out of his net.

"Excuse me, Fisherman Kee," Yum Yung shouted. "Have you seen my missing bagel?"

Fisherman Kee threw his net back into the water with a splash. "Bagel? What in the salty sea is a bagel?"

"It is round and it has a hole in the middle," Yum Yung explained.

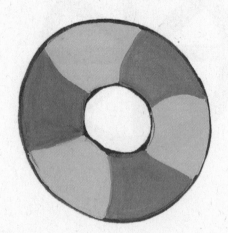

"Oh," Fisherman Kee said with a nod. He pointed to his life ring floating below. "Is that a bagel?"

Yum Yung frowned. "No, that is not my bagel."

"I am sorry, Yum Yung," Fisherman Kee said. "I know about fish that swim in the sea, but I know nothing about bagels."

253

Next Yum Yung visited Beekeeper Lee, who was collecting honey from a beehive.

"Excuse me, Beekeeper Lee," Yum Yung hollered from a distance. "Have you seen my missing bagel?"

Beekeeper Lee raised her bee veil. "Bagel? What in the sweet name of honey is a bagel?"

"It is round and it has a hole in the middle," Yum Yung explained.

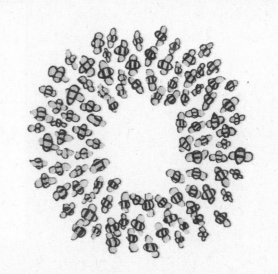

"Ah," Beekeeper Lee said with a nod. She pointed to the thick swarm of bees circling over her head. "Is that a bagel?"

Yum Yung frowned. "No, that is not my bagel."

"I am sorry, Yum Yung," Beekeeper Lee said. "I know about the buzzing business of bees, but I know nothing about bagels."

Yum Yung sat down on a quiet hillside
and moaned. All hope for a bagel seemed lost!
    Then a delicious smell tickled his nose. He
sniffed curiously. Where was it coming from?
    Yum Yung looked into the valley and
blinked with delight.
There was Oh's Heavenly Bakery!

Yum Yung rushed into Oh's Heavenly Bakery, where Baker Oh was making one of her famous rice cakes.

"Baker Oh," Yum Yung pleaded, "please tell me you have my missing bagel!"

Baker Oh sprinkled a few pine nuts on the rice cake. "Bagel? What in a baker's kitchen is a bagel?"

"It is round, and it has a hole in the middle," Yum Yung explained.

"I am very sorry, Yum Yung," Baker Oh said. "I have not seen your missing bagel. But maybe that pigeon tapping at the window has better news for you."

Baker Oh opened the window. The bird flew in and landed on Yum Yung's shoulder—with a message!

While Baker Oh fed the pigeon rice cake crumbs, Yum Yung read the message aloud.

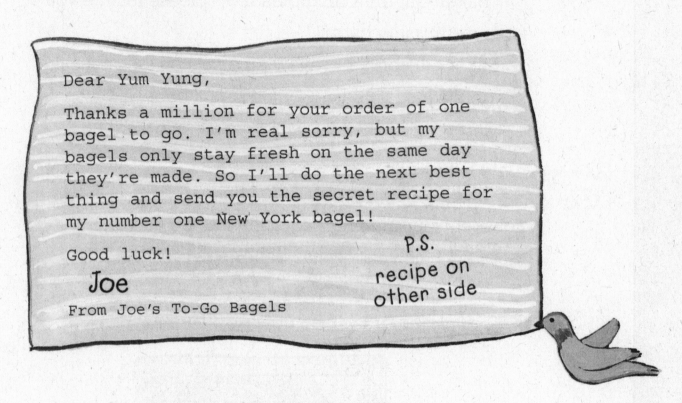

Dear Yum Yung,

Thanks a million for your order of one bagel to go. I'm real sorry, but my bagels only stay fresh on the same day they're made. So I'll do the next best thing and send you the secret recipe for my number one New York bagel!

Good luck!

Joe

From Joe's To-Go Bagels

P.S.
recipe on other side

Baker Oh studied the recipe, then frowned.

"I am afraid I do not have all the special ingredients to make a New York bagel, Yum Yung. My sweet rice cakes are made with rice, sugar, and water. This bagel calls for flour, sea salt, and honey."

Yum Yung jumped. "Did you say flour, sea salt, and honey?"

"Yes," Baker Oh replied.

"I will return!" Yum Yung promised.

And indeed he did return—with Farmer Ahn and Fisherman Kee and Beekeeper Lee.

"I have the flour!" exclaimed Farmer Ahn.

"I have the sea salt!" exclaimed Fisherman Kee.

"And I have the honey!" exclaimed Beekeeper Lee.

It was time to make a New York bagel!

Baker Oh tied an apron around Yum Yung's waist. Following the recipe, Yum Yung instructed Farmer Ahn to sift flour into a mixing bowl. He instructed Fisherman Kee to sprinkle in the sea salt. He instructed Beekeeper Lee to spoon in the golden honey. Then Baker Oh poured in the water and tossed in a pinch of yeast.

271

Yum Yung kneaded the fragrant dough and formed it into a ring shape. He perfected the edges, especially for the hole in the middle. He dropped the dough into a large pot of simmering water. Minutes later, it floated to the top.

Then Yum Yung sprinkled it with sesame seeds, and into the oven it went.

Yum Yung watched the dough magically puff higher and higher until it nearly filled the whole oven—until it was a golden brown bagel!

The bagel was so big that Farmer Ahn, Fisherman Kee, Beekeeper Lee, and Baker Oh had to help Yum Yung carry it out of Oh's Heavenly Bakery. They all grunted as they set the bagel down under a persimmon tree on the quiet hillside. Yum Yung broke off a piece of the bagel for each of his friends.

"Hmm!" said Farmer Ahn.

"Oh!" said Fisherman Kee.

"Ah!" said Beekeeper Lee.

"Mmm!" said Baker Oh.

263

The moment had finally come for Yum Yung to eat his New York bagel.

He closed his eyes and took his first bite. It was a perfect bagel with a hint of honey so sweet it made him sigh. It was soft and plump and chewy and delicious all in one bite. It was so heavenly he could even taste the curious hole in the middle!

Yum Yung declared:

"At last I have my bagel!"

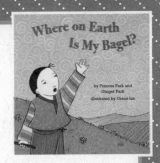

Turn and Talk

Use details from *Where on Earth Is My Bagel?* to answer these questions with a partner.

1. **Make Inferences** Yum Yung decides that his bagel must be lost. What does he do next? What does that tell you about Yum Yung?

2. What is the setting? How is the setting important to the story events?

3. How do the people in Yum Yung's community work together to solve his problem?

Talking Tip

Complete the sentence to ask your partner for more information about an answer.

Could you tell me more about _____ ?

Cite Text Evidence

Write a Story

PROMPT How would the pigeon tell the story? How is the pigeon's point of view different from the other characters'? Use details from the words and pictures to explain your ideas.

PLAN First, draw or write what happens first, next, and last from the pigeon's point of view.

First

Next

Last

WRITE Now write the pigeon's version of the story. Include details that tell what the pigeon sees, does, hears, and feels. Remember to:

- Tell the story events in order.

- Use the words *I* and *me* to write in the pigeon's voice.

_____

_____

_____

_____

_____

_____

_____

_____

_____

_____

USA England Sweden

Prepare to Read

GENRE STUDY ▶ **Narrative nonfiction** gives facts about a topic, but it reads like a story. As you read *May Day Around the World*, pay attention to:

- main topic and details
- real settings
- dialogue, or what the characters in the story say

SET A PURPOSE ▶ Make a good guess, or **prediction,** about what the text will be about. Use the text features, like headings, to help you predict. Read to see if you are right. If not, make a new prediction.

POWER WORDS
trunk
races
clutched
forgot

Build Background: May Day

Hawaii
USA France

May Day

Around the World

by Tori Telfer

illustrated by Lynne Avril

Uppsala, Sweden

Gustaf has never been up this late! He watches his father throw another piece of old furniture on the bonfire. Tonight they are celebrating Walpurgis Eve, the last day before spring.

Gustaf's neighbors sing soft songs around the fire. His mother brings him a green blanket and a bowl of nettle soup. "Spring is coming in the morning," she whispers.

Gustaf curls up on the blanket and feels the lovely warmth of the fire.

Austin, TX, USA

Maria and Carlos put a May Day basket on Ms. Garcia's doorstep. The basket is filled with purple violets and a chocolate bar.

Maria rings the doorbell, and they run behind a big oak tree. *Creak!* The door is opening!

Maria peeks out from behind the trunk. "Happy May Day, Ms. Garcia!"

Paris, France

Adèle races through the park with a coin clutched in her hand. May Day is her favorite time of year. Everyone is wearing bright colors, and the birds are just starting to sing.

"One lily of the valley, *s'il vous plaît*," she says to the man selling flowers.

Adèle runs back to her grandfather and puts the flower in his buttonhole. "*Joyeux premier mai, Papi!*" she says.

"Happy May Day, Grandpa!"

272

Wailea, Hawaii, USA

A'ala helps her aunt Malia get ready for the Lei Day parade. Her aunt has been crowned Lei Queen!

"How do I look?" asks her aunt.

"You forgot something," says A'ala. She slips a long, delicate lei of ilima blossoms over her aunt's head. The lei smells sweet and fresh, just like springtime.

"Now *you* forgot something!" says her aunt Malia. "Giving a lei means you get a kiss."

273

Peasmarsh, England

Annabelle and Edward are dancing around the Maypole. They've been practicing for weeks! If they get the steps just right, the ribbons will wind around the pole in a beautiful crisscross pattern. Annabelle wears her new white dress and yellow ribbon in her hair, the color of the first spring daisies. Edward is dressed as "The Green Man," full of mischief.

Oh, no! Edward's dog, Sammy, is running toward the Maypole. He wants to dance, too!

Watch out, Edward!

274

Use details from *May Day Around the World* to answer these questions with a partner.

1. **Make and Confirm Predictions** How did using the headings and other text features help you make predictions before and as you read? What were you right about? What was different?

2. Compare two of the May Day celebrations. How are they alike and different?

3. What was the author's purpose for writing this text?

Listening Tip

Look at your partner. Listen politely and find out what your partner is saying.

Write a Description

PROMPT If you could go to one celebration from *May Day
Around the World*, which one would you choose? What would it
be like? Use details from the text and illustrations to explain
your ideas.

PLAN First, fill in the web with four details about the holiday.

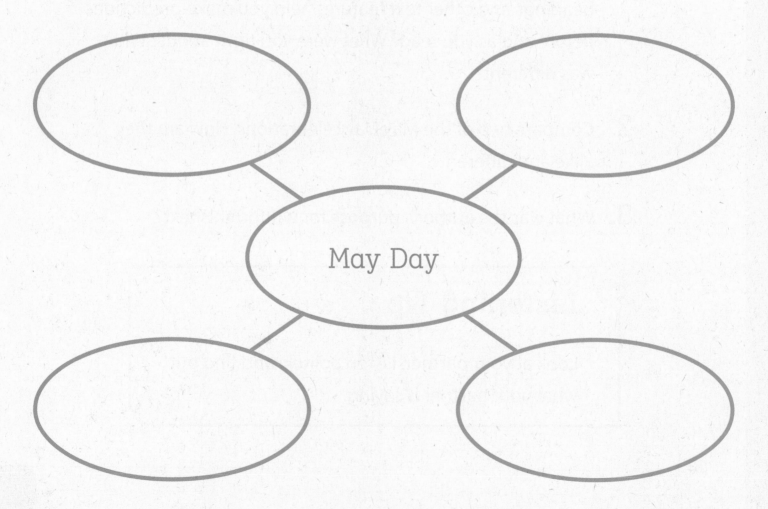

May Day

WRITE Now, write a description of the May Day celebration you would like to attend. Tell what you would see, hear, taste, and do. Remember to:

- Use words that paint a picture of the celebration.

- Capitalize the name of the holiday.

_____

_____

_____

_____

_____

_____

_____

_____

_____

Prepare to Read

GENRE STUDY **Informational text** is nonfiction. It gives facts about a topic. As you read *Goal!*, pay attention to:

• details and facts about a topic

• facts about the world

• photographs

SET A PURPOSE As you read, **make connections** to find ways that the text is like other texts you have read and things in your own life. Compare and contrast to help you understand and remember the text.

Meet Sean Taylor.

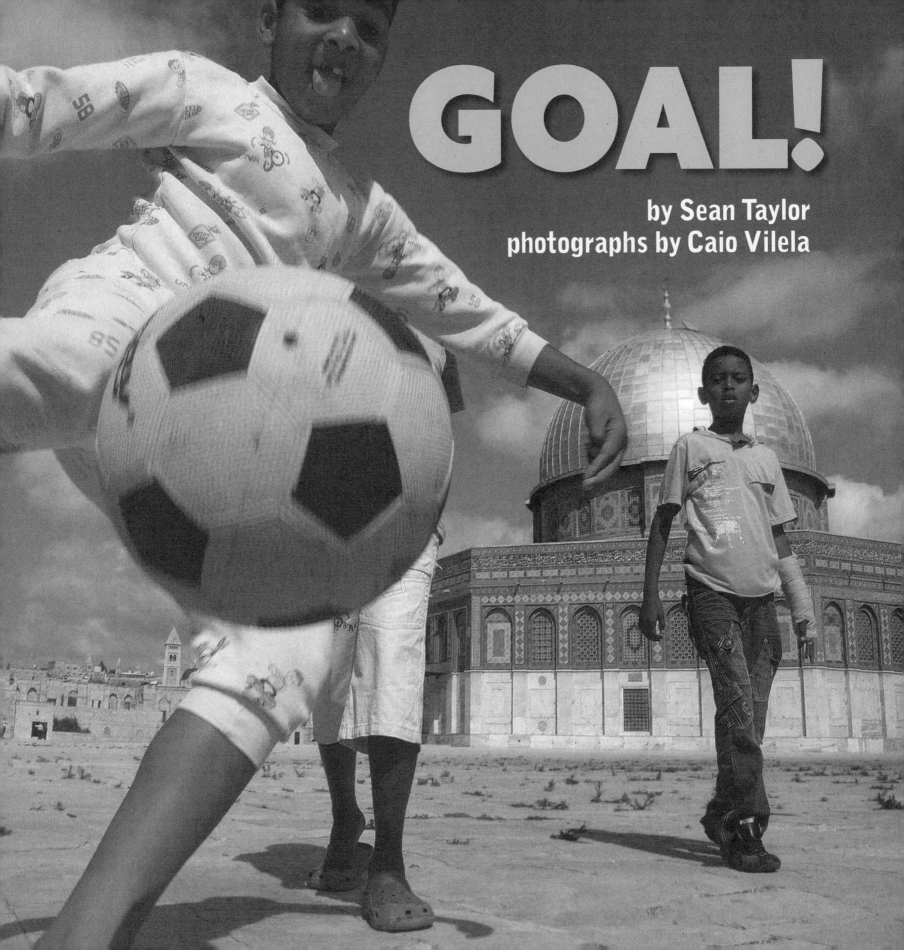

GOAL!

by Sean Taylor
photographs by Caio Vilela

Brazil

Where there's a ball, there will always be someone who wants to play soccer.

U.S.A.

When you play soccer, you're not allowed to use your arms and hands unless you are the goalkeeper.

But you can use the rest of your body—your feet, your legs, your hips, your chest, and your head.

There are more than 6,000 different languages spoken on our planet. But children all over the world understand soccer.

In some sports, teams can score up to 100 points in a game. In a soccer game you don't get many goals. Sometimes you don't get any at all. You have to be patient. So when a goal comes, it's special!

Spain

England

When the ball comes your way, you might feel excited, you might feel calm, you might even feel a bit scared.

Playing soccer teaches you lots of things—how to be quick, how to be clever, how to see what's going on around you, and how to be brave.

You can play soccer almost anywhere—in a garden, down an alley, on a playground, in a park, or on a beach.

You don't need to buy anything to play soccer. You can make goalposts with two stones, two sticks, or two shirts.

If you don't have a real soccer ball, you can make one with rolled-up socks, newspaper, and string, or even an orange in a plastic bag.

Some people invent machines. Some people invent medicines. And some people invent tricks with soccer balls.

When you trick a defender by pretending to go one way and then send the player after an imaginary ball, it's called a step-over. When you throw yourself in the air and kick the ball over your head, it's called a bicycle kick.

Jordan

Iran

Every soccer game is like a story. It's full of characters, emotions, and drama.

And no one knows how it will end until the final whistle blows.

There's nothing quite like the excitement before you start a game of soccer. Anything can happen!

At the end of the game, you may have won or you may have lost. But you can lose a game and still play your very best. And that is a kind of winning.

Pakistan

284

Nepal

Soccer is not about showing off how well you can play.
It's about showing how well you can play for your team.
The best players don't worry about being the stars of
their teams. They want their teams to be the stars.

The ball doesn't care if you're big or small. It doesn't care what your religion is, what race you are, or where you come from. It doesn't even care if you're good at soccer.

Anyone can play soccer—anywhere in the world.

You can have fun playing soccer with just one friend or even on your own.

China

New Zealand

No other sport brings people together like soccer. No other sport is played by so many people in so many different countries. When you are playing soccer, there will always be someone else playing, somewhere in the world.

Soccer Around the World

Soccer is played all over the world! And in most other countries—except Canada and the U.S.A.—it is called football. Here are the countries mentioned in this book and the year each country's first national soccer team was founded.

USA
1913

ENGLAND
1863

PAKISTAN
1948

CHINA
1924

SPAIN
1913

IRAN
1920

NEPAL
1951

BRAZIL
1914

JORDAN
1949

NEW ZEALAND
1891

Turn and Talk

Use details from *Goal!* to answer these questions with a partner.

1. **Make Connections** Compare and contrast *Goal!* and *May Day Around the World*. How are the texts alike and different?

2. Look back at pages 286–287. What is the main idea of this section? What does the author want readers to understand about soccer?

3. How can you use the map on page 288 to find and understand information about soccer?

Talking Tip

Use details from the text to explain your ideas. Complete the sentence below.

I think _____ because _____.

Write an Opinion

PROMPT What do you think it takes to be a great soccer player? Use details in the words and photographs to explain your ideas.

PLAN First, think of qualities a person would need to be a great soccer player. Write or draw them below.

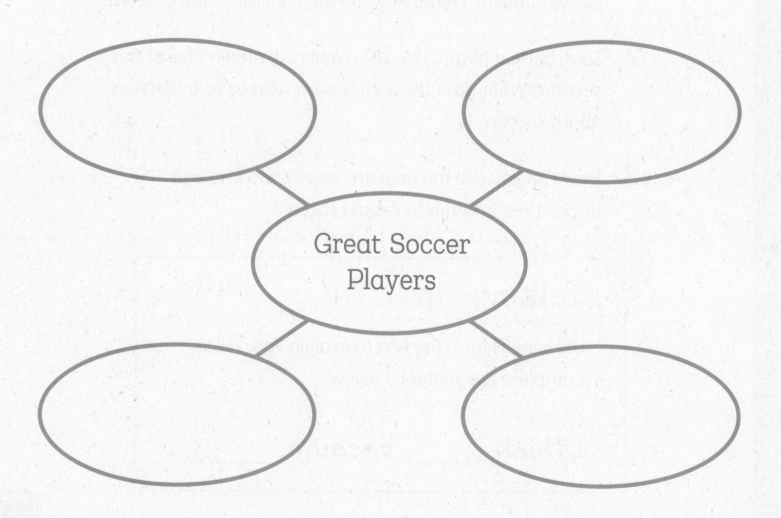

Great Soccer Players

WRITE Now write your opinion. Tell what qualities you think a person should have to be a great soccer player. Remember to:

- Be sure to explain your opinion with reasons.

- Include details that support your reasons.

_____

_____

_____

_____

_____

_____

_____

_____

_____

_____

Prepare to Read

GENRE STUDY **Poetry** uses images, sounds, and rhythm to express feelings. As you read *Poems in the Attic*, look at:

- how the poem makes you feel
- patterns of sounds, words, or lines
- words that appeal to the senses

SET A PURPOSE As you read, **make connections** by finding ways that this text is like things in your life and other texts you have read. This will help you understand and remember the text.

POWER WORDS

stacked

flitting

leave

breathless

mound

shuffled

clamber

adventures

Meet Nikki Grimes.

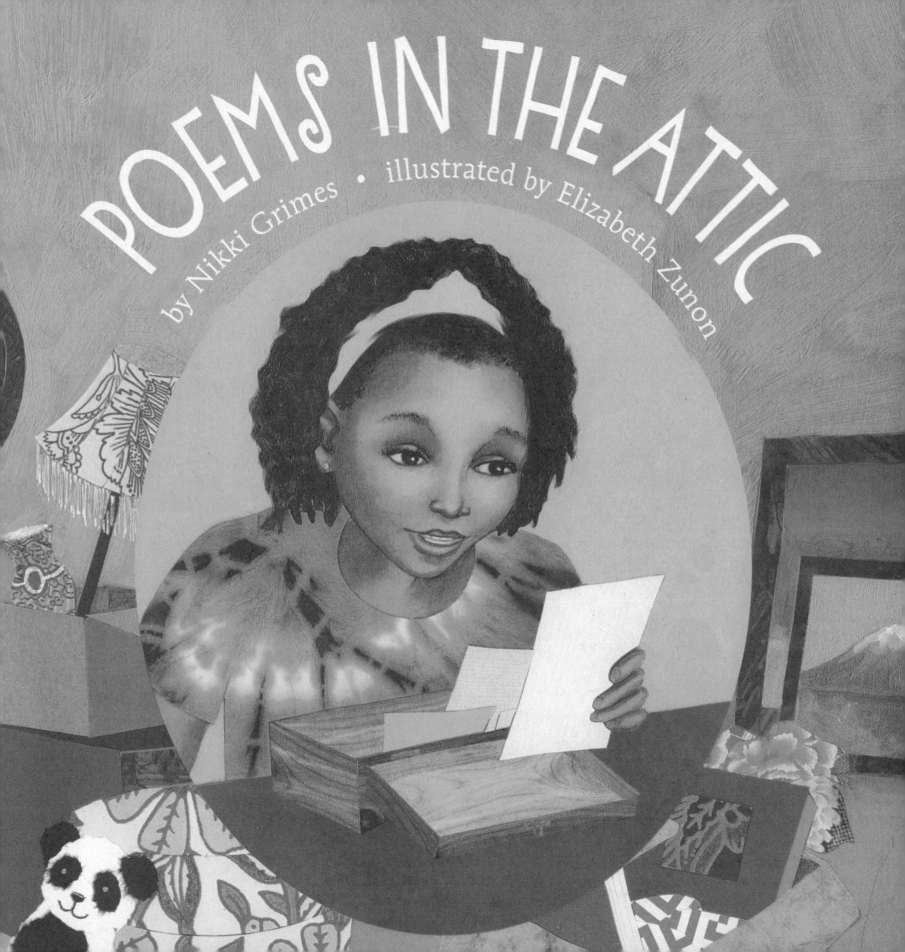

Poems in the Attic

Grandma's attic is stacked with secrets.
Last visit, I found poems Mama wrote
before I was born, before I was even imagined.
She started when she was seven—same age as me!

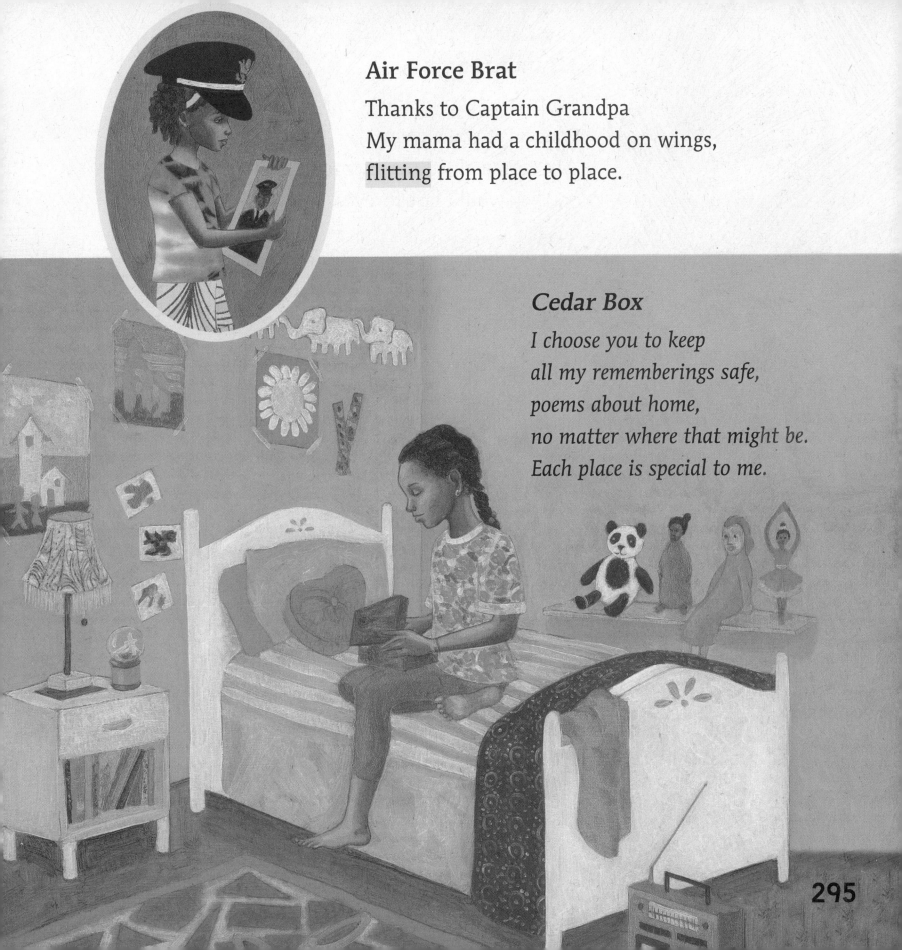

Air Force Brat

Thanks to Captain Grandpa
My mama had a childhood on wings,
flitting from place to place.

Cedar Box

I choose you to keep
all my rememberings safe,
poems about home,
no matter where that might be.
Each place is special to me.

Grandma Says

Memories can be like sandcastles
the waves wash away.
My mama glued her memories with words
so they would last forever.

Cabrillo Beach
CALIFORNIA

Home on leave, Daddy
took me to the Grunion Run!
Our flashlights found them—
slim fish, silver as new dimes,
wiggling ashore to lay eggs.

296

Bedtime

Grandma sings me to sleep
with one of Mama's poems.
I dream of skies
my mother's eyes have seen.

Aurora Borealis
ALASKA

*My brother and me
held hands, breathless, as we watched
this dancing rainbow
shimmy 'cross Alaska's sky
in a skirt of night and light.*

Paper Candleholders

Next day, Grandma lays out paper bags,
scissors, and paint, teaching me
a kind of magic she and Mama used to make
every December, in New Mexico.

Luminarias
NEW MEXICO

*I scalloped the tops,
Mom painted happy faces.
After we were done,
our brown bag candleholders
bloomed bright, lighting up the night.*

298

Who Is She?
It's funny to think of Mama
making a mess with arts and crafts
or playing, sand in her hair,
giggling like a kid—like me!

White Sands National Monument
NEW MEXICO

I scaled the first dune,
brother close behind. On three,
we rolled down the mound,
tumbling in sand and laughter,
ready to do it again.

Snow Dream

I flip through old photos of Mama,
smile at the snowman that stands
taller than she. I never get to see
snow where we live.

Colorado Springs
COLORADO

Dad came home with skis
short as my little-girl legs.
I strapped them on tight,
shuffled across the backyard,
flying downhill—in my dreams.

300

Imagine

Three days of not seeing my mama
feels like forever.
I bet she used to miss her dad,
gone for months.

Garden of the Gods
COLORADO

*On Bring Your Dad Day,
I brought along a photo
of the two of us
at the Garden of the Gods.
I clutched my photo, wishing . . . .*

Boys

Guys at school tease me
for collecting rocks "like a boy."
Next time, I'll tell them to
gather sharks' teeth "like a girl"!

Cherry Point
NORTH CAROLINA

Any day's perfect
for walking the river's edge.
I slipped over rocks,
gathered bruises and sharks' teeth
to show Dad when he's on leave.

302

Sailing

Pictures of kayaks and canoes
swim on the blue of our walls
thanks to Mama, who buys them all.
Now I think I know why.

Accotink Bay
VIRGINIA

The bay called us three.
We silently kayaked near
the bird-breeding box.
If only Dad would let us
clamber atop it and dance!

303

City Slicker

We've lived in the city
long as I can remember,
but Mama is always going on about
nature and the wonders of the woods.

Brackenridge Park
TEXAS

Dad says I'm lucky.
Mom sent me horseback riding
in the morning mist,
and as it cleared, I spotted
a great, green heron lift, soar!

Chopsticks

At dinner I ask Grandma
for the chopsticks Mama
taught me to use. Once, I asked Mama
where she learned, and she just smiled.

Cherry Blossoms

JAPAN

Spring! Kimono time.
I joined the parade of girls
strolling avenues
dusted with cherry blossoms.
I caught a few, like snowflakes.

305

Tent

I set up a tent
in Grandma's backyard,
take a flashlight so I can read.
Mama's poems and me go camping.

Class Trip

JAPAN

My class camping trip!
Rhinoceros beetles and
dragonflies joined us.
We ate squid-on-a-stick, slept
at the foot of Mount Fuji.

306

Moving Day

I don't know how she did it,
moving all the time.
I get dizzy thinking about
all those good-byes.

Station Next

PORTUGAL

Move Number—who knows?
We call them all adventures.
I pack my poems,
wishing I could fold my friends
and slip them in my suitcase.

Endings

Grandma calls me to dinner,
but I read Mama's last poem
one more time.

Pride

WASHINGTON, DC, AREA

My heart dances when
Air Force One flings its shadow
across our front porch.
Dad promises we'll see this
countless times, because we're home.

Time to Go

Mama comes for me tomorrow.
I have a surprise for her.
I've been busy writing
poems of my own.

Let's See

Pencil and paper,
hole punch and ribbon—all set.
I work past bedtime,
copy Mama's poems, then
stitch them together with mine.

Back to the Attic

I put Mama's poems back in the chest
where I found them
and leave a stack of mine
for someone else to find.

The Gift

I run to Mama,
tackle her with hugs, kisses,
then hand her the book.
Breathlessly, I wait for her
to unwrap our memories.

Use details from *Poems in the Attic* to answer these questions with a partner.

1. **Make Connections** Describe a time you visited somewhere you had never been before. How does that experience help you understand the characters in this text?

2. What does the girl mean when she says, "I dream of skies my mother's eyes have seen"?

3. These poems tell two stories. Who is the narrator of each story? How are their stories alike and different?

Listening Tip

You learn from others by listening carefully. Think about what your partner says and what you learn.

Write a Memory Poem

PROMPT The main character says that her mama glued her
memories with words so they would last forever. Think of a
memory you would like to remember forever. How would you
describe it in a poem?

PLAN First, make a chart. On one side, write details about your
special memory. On the other side, write words with interesting
sounds that describe each detail. Look back at the text for ideas.

Details	Words

WRITE Now write your poem using the best words on your chart. Remember to:

- Use words that paint a picture of your topic.

- Think about how the words in your poem sound together.

_____

_____

_____

_____

_____

_____

_____

_____

_____

_____

Prepare to View

GENRE STUDY ▶ **Videos** are short movies that give you information or something for you to watch for enjoyment. As you watch *What's for Lunch Around the World?*, notice:

- how pictures, sounds, and words work together
- information about the topic
- the purpose of the video

SET A PURPOSE ▶ Some videos use **graphic features** in the same way that print books do. As you view, think about how these features help you find information quickly in the video.

Build Background: Favorite Foods

What's for Lunch Around the World?

As You View Discover what's for lunch today! Look carefully at the pictures. Watch for the labels that pop up. How do the words and pictures work together to show you what people all around the world eat for lunch?

Turn and Talk

Use details from *What's for Lunch Around the World?* to answer these questions with a partner.

1. **Graphic Features** How can you use the labels to understand more about each lunch?

2. What are some things that the lunches have in common?

3. Which of the lunches would you most like to eat? Which food are you most curious to try? Use details from the video to explain your opinions.

Talking Tip

Add your own idea to what your partner says. Be sure to be polite.

I like your idea. My idea is _____.

Let's Wrap Up!

? Essential Question

What can we learn from different people and cultures?

Pick one of these activities to show what you have learned about the topic.

1. Why Study Cultures?

Write a paragraph to explain why it is important to learn about people and traditions from different parts of the world. Use details from the texts to explain your opinion.

Word Challenge

Can you use the word harmony in your opinion?

318

2. Collage of Cultures!

Think about the texts you read. What do they teach you about how people share their cultures with others? Draw or find pictures that show what you've learned. Then make a collage. Add labels to describe your pictures. Share your collage with a partner.

My Notes

Glossary

A

account [ə-kount'] An account is a report of something that happened. My teacher gave an **account** of his trip.

achieve [ə-chēv'] When you achieve something, you get it after a lot of hard work. You can **achieve** your goal if you work hard.

adorable [ə-dôr'ə-bəl] Something adorable is cute and easy to love. That little lamb is **adorable**!

adventures [ăd-věn'chərz] Adventures are exciting experiences. We have many fun **adventures** together.

allowed [ə-loud'] When you are allowed to do something, it is all right for you to do it. We are **allowed** to have a snack now.

alone [ə-lōn'] When you do something alone, you do it by yourself. I went for a quiet walk **alone** on the trail.

approached [ə-prōcht'] If someone approached you, that person got closer to you. The dog **approached** us slowly.

arrange [ə-rānj'] If you arrange things, you put them in a certain order. Please **arrange** the boxes by size.

arrive [ə-rīv'] When you arrive, you get to a place. Grandma and Grandpa were very happy to see us **arrive** for a visit.

ashamed [ə-shāmd'] When you are ashamed, you feel bad about something you have done. He was **ashamed** that he lost the money.

attached [ə-tăcht'] When things are attached, they are joined together. These papers are **attached** with a staple.

attack [ə-tăk'] If you attack something, you try to hurt or damage it. The cat tried to **attack** a mouse.

B

breathless [brĕth′lĭs]   If you are breathless, you have a hard time catching your breath. I was **breathless** after running up the hill.

C

clamber [klăm′bər, klăm′ər]   When you clamber, you climb quickly using your hands and feet. We **clamber** up the rocks to reach the top.

clutched [klŭcht]   If you clutched something, you held it tightly. Tyler **clutched** his father's hand.

coast [kōst]   The coast is the land that is next to the sea. We love walking along the **coast**.

communicate [kə-myo͞o′nĭ-kāt′]   When you communicate, you share information or ideas. Sign language is one way to **communicate**.

crack [krăk]   Crack means to break or split. You have to **crack** the coconut open to eat it.

crouches [krouch′ĭz]   When something crouches, it bends its legs and lowers its body. The tiger **crouches** in the tall grass.

culture [kŭl′chər]   A group's culture is the ideas and beliefs the people share. Making this special meal together is an important part of my family's **culture**.

current [kûr′ənt, kŭr′ənt]   If something is current, it is happening in the present time. I have a **current** issue of the magazine.

D

dared [dârd]   If you dared to do something, you were brave enough to do it. We **dared** to jump into the cold water.

darting [därt′ĭng]   If something is darting, it is moving from place to place very quickly. We saw a deer **darting** across the street.

deal [dēl]   You deal with people by understanding and getting along with them. I know how to **deal** with a crying baby.

delight [dĭ-līt′]   Delight is great joy. Being together filled us all with **delight**.

deserved [dĭ-zûrvd′]   If you deserved something, you earned it because of something you did. They **deserved** to take home the trophy.

E

ecosystem [ē′kō-sĭs′təm, ĕk′ō-sĭs′təm]   An ecosystem is all the animals and plants that live in the same area. A pond is one type of **ecosystem**.

elders [ĕl′dərz]   Elders are people who are older than you. She loved hearing stories from her **elders**.

extra [ĕk′strə]   An extra amount of something is more than usual. I took an **extra** glass of juice for my friend.

F

fertilize [fûr′tl-īz′]   When you fertilize soil, you add something that helps plants grow. **Fertilize** the soil before you plant seeds.

figured [fĭg′yərd]   If you figured out something, you came to understand it. Robbie **figured** out how to solve the problem.

final [fī′nəl]   In a group of events, the **final** one is the last one. Today is the **final** day of the sale.

flitting [flĭt′ĭng]   If you are flitting, you are moving quickly from place to place. Two birds were **flitting** from tree to tree.

flock [flŏk]   A flock is a group of birds. We saw a **flock** of geese in the pond.

forgot [fər-gŏt′, fôr-gŏt′]   If you forgot something, you did not remember it. I **forgot** to pack my homework.

founded [found′ĭd]   The date when something was founded was when it was started or created. The camp was **founded** five years ago.

fragrant [frā′grənt]   Something fragrant smells sweet. I smelled the **fragrant** flowers.

fuels [fyo͞o′əlz]   Something that fuels another thing gives it power. Healthy food **fuels** the body.

G

germinate [jûr′mə-nāt′]   Seeds germinate when they begin to grow. The seeds began to **germinate** this week.

glanced [glănsd]   If you glanced at something, you looked at it quickly. I **glanced** at my watch while I walked.

growled [grould]   If something growled, it made a deep, angry sound. My stomach **growled** before lunch.

grumpy [grŭm′pē]   Someone who is grumpy is in a bad mood. Val was **grumpy** because she missed her favorite show.

grunted [grŭnt′ĭd]   If you grunted, you made a low, deep sound. He **grunted** as he tried to lift the heavy chair.

H

habitat [hăb′ĭ-tăt′]   A habitat is a place where plants and animals live and grow. We saw an elephant in its natural **habitat**.

harmony [här′mə-nē]   Being in harmony means living together in a peaceful way. My family lives in **harmony** together.

hauling [hôl′ĭng]   When you are hauling something heavy, you are pulling it hard. We are **hauling** our wagon up the hill.

heritage [hĕr′ĭ-tĭj]   A country's heritage is its way of doing things that is passed down over time. We learned about our family **heritage** from Grandpa.

hide [hīd]   A hide is an animal's skin. The shoes are made of animal **hide**.

hollered [hŏl'ərd]   If you hollered, you shouted loudly. We **hollered** as loudly as we could.

hurdle [hûr'dl]   A hurdle is a problem that could stop you from doing something. Eliza leapt over each **hurdle** and was the first person to cross the finish line.

I

imaginary [ĭ-măj'ə-nĕr'ē]   Something that is imaginary only happens in your mind. He wrote a story about an **imaginary** world with talking animals.

J

joking [jōk'ĭng]   If you are joking, you are saying something to be funny. I was **joking** with my friends at the slumber party.

L

leave [lēv]   A leave is time away from work. I am so happy that my father is home on **leave** now.

M

minerals [mĭn'ər-əlz]   Minerals are natural substances that do not come from plants or animals. The soil has **minerals** in it.

mingles [mĭng'gəlz]   When something mingles with another thing, the two things mix together. The new camper **mingles** with other children at camp.

moisten [moi'sən]   When you moisten something, you wet it a little. **Moisten** a sponge before washing the dishes.

motioned [mō'shənd]   If you motioned, you moved your hand or head to show someone what to do. The museum guide **motioned** for us to follow her.

mound [mound] A mound is a hill or pile. There was a **mound** of dirt next to the house while it was under construction.

N

nasty [năs'tē] When something is nasty, it is very unpleasant. I have a **nasty** scrape on my knee, but I will be ready to play by this weekend.

nod [nŏd] A nod is when you move your head up and down to show that you agree. She gave me a **nod** and kept talking.

O

offered [ô'fərd, ŏf'ərd] If you offered something to someone, you asked to give it to him or her. She **offered** her teacher an apple.

overflowing [ō'vər-flō'ĭng] If something is overflowing, no more can fit in it. The glass was **overflowing** with water.

oversized [ō'vər-sīzd'] Something oversized is very big. My father gave me an **oversized** shirt that I will grow into someday.

P

patient [pā'shənt] If you are patient, you can wait for something without complaining. I am **patient** with my baby brother.

plenty [plĕn'tē] When you have plenty, you have a lot of something. We have **plenty** of food for everyone.

poke [pōk] If something jabs into you suddenly, it is said to poke you. Be careful not to **poke** yourself with the nails.

potential [pə-tĕn'shəl] Potential is what you can do in the future if you work hard now. I have the **potential** to be a great swimmer.

prances [prăns′ĭz]   When something prances, it moves by taking high steps. The beautiful horse **prances** in the snow.

prickles [prĭk′əlz]   Prickles are small points that stick out. The plant was covered with **prickles**.

pride [prīd]   When you feel pride, you are pleased about something you did well. He spoke with **pride** about his work.

process [prŏs′ĕs′, prō′sĕs′]   A process is a series of steps that happen in order. Writing a book can be a long **process**.

provides [prə-vīdz′]   Provides means to give something that is needed. The school **provides** pencils for students.

R

races [rās′ĭz]   Someone who races runs or moves very fast. She **races** outside to catch the bus.

reminding [rĭ-mīnd′ĭng]   If you are reminding people, you are telling them again. This string on my finger is **reminding** me to water the garden.

route [rōōt, rout]   A route is the path someone takes to get from place to place. We will take the quickest **route** to the concert hall for the big show.

S

secret [sē′krĭt]   When something is secret, very few people know about it. Kim had a funny **secret** to share.

seedlings [sēd′lĭngz]   Seedlings are young plants that grow from seeds. The **seedlings** are growing taller.

selfless [sĕlf′lĭs]   If you are selfless, you care more about others than yourself. My friend is **selfless** and likes to help others.

sensitive [sĕn′sĭ-tĭv]   If something is sensitive, it is quick to respond to something else. Some people are **sensitive** to the cold.

series [sîr′ēz]   A series is a group of things that come one after another. I read the whole **series** of books.

sharp [shärp]   If something is sharp, it has an edge that can cut you. The scissors were very **sharp**.

sheltered [shĕl′tərd]   A sheltered place protects from wind and rain. The cave was a **sheltered** place.

shrugged [shrŭgd]   If you shrugged, you lifted and lowered your shoulders to show you did not know. He **shrugged** his shoulders when I asked if he thought it would rain.

shuffled [shŭf′əld]   If you shuffled, you walked slowly and dragged your feet. I heard crunching sounds as I **shuffled** through the fallen leaves.

slippery [slĭp′ə-rē]   Something slippery is wet, smooth, and hard to hold. The road was **slippery** after the rain.

smothered [smŭth′ərd]   Something that is smothered is thickly covered with something else. The delicious toast was **smothered** with butter and strawberry jam.

species [spē′shēz, spē′sēz]   A species is a group of animals or plants that are alike. The nature center had many **species** of frogs.

spiky [spī′kē]   Something spiky has sharp points. This tree has **spiky** leaves.

sprout [sprout]   When plants sprout, they begin to grow. The plant will **sprout** leaves.

stacked [stăkt]   If you stacked things, you placed them on top of other things. I **stacked** the boxes in the garage.

starlit [stär′lĭt′]   A starlit place gets its light from the stars. We took a walk under a pretty **starlit** sky.

statements [stāt′mənts]   Statements are words or sentences that people said or wrote to share information. I agree with your **statements** about being on time and working hard.

stubborn [stŭb′ərn]   Someone who is stubborn does not want to change. My cousin is **stubborn** and will not change his mind.

surface [sûr′fəs]   The surface of something is the top or outside of it. The beautiful fish swam up to the **surface** of the pond to be fed.

survive [sər-vīv′]   When things survive, they stay alive. Animals and plants need water to **survive**.

swipe [swīp]   If you swipe something, you take it. I did not **swipe** your candy.

T

thorns [thôrnz]   Thorns are points that grow on a branch or stem. This plant has many **thorns**.

timeline [tīm′līn′]   A timeline is a visual that shows events in the order they happened. This **timeline** tells us information about the history of communication.

trills [trĭlz]   When a bird trills, it sings and chirps. The bird **trills** near my window.

trunk [trŭngk]   A trunk is the main part of a tree from which branches grow. The very old tree had a huge **trunk** that many of us could hide behind.

tucked [tŭkt]   If you tucked something, you pushed it behind or into something else. He **tucked** his shirt into his pants.

W

weary [wîr′ē]   Someone who is weary is very tired. We were all beginning to feel **weary** as we got closer to the finish line.

whacked [wăkt, hwăkt]   If you whacked something, you hit it hard. Winston **whacked** the ball with all his might, and he got his very first home run.

whimpered [wĭm′pərd, hwĭm′pərd]   If you whimpered, you made a quiet, crying noise. The dog **whimpered** when it was home alone.

whir [wûr, hwûr]   A whir is a buzzing or humming sound. When we heard the **whir** of the mixer, we knew Mom was making us cookies.

wit [wĭt]   Wit is a talent for using words to be funny. These books are full of **wit**.

wobbly [wŏb′lē]   Something that is wobbly is moving from side to side in a shaky way. The newborn donkey was **wobbly** on his feet.

wraps [răps]   If something wraps around another thing, it winds or goes around that thing. He **wraps** a blanket around himself to keep warm.

Index of Titles and Authors

Abuelo and the Three Bears **212**

Ada, Alma Flor **208**

At Home in the Wild **198**

Blanco, Alberto **207**

Bruchac, James **50**

Campoy, F. Isabel **208**

Don't Touch Me! **144**

Drum Dream Girl **64**

Ducklings Jump from Nest **232**

Engle, Margarita **64**

Experiment with What a Plant Needs to Grow **102**

Gillin, Boyd N. **40**

Goal! **278**

Great Innovators: George Washington Carver **154**

Grimes, Nikki **292**

Higgins, Nadia **102**

How to Make a Timeline **40**

I Am Helen Keller **8**

Jack and the Beanstalk **116**

Jackie and the Beanstalk **130**

Lester, Helen **116**

Long, Long Journey, The **166**

Markle, Sandra **166**

May Day Around the World **268**

Meltzer, Brad **8**

Mortensen, Lori **130**

Owen, Ruth **184**

Park, Frances and Ginger **244**

Poems in the Attic **292**

Preston, Elizabeth **144**

Roberto Clemente **90**

Sea Otter Pups **184**

Sidman, Joyce **202**

Spinelli, Eileen **200**

Stories He Tells, The: The Story of Joseph Bruchac, **50**

Taylor, Sean **278**

Telfer, Tori **268**

Tello, Jerry 212

What's for Lunch Around the
   World? 314

Where on Earth Is My Bagel? 244

Acknowledgments

Abuelo and the Three Bears/Abuelo y los tres osos by Jerry Tello, illustrated by Ana López Escrivá. Text copyright ©1997 by Jerry Tello. Illustrations copyright ©1997 by Ana López Escrivá. Reprinted by permission of Houghton Mifflin Harcourt Publishing Company.

"The Ant" from *Mamá Goose: A Latino Nursery Treasure* by Alma Flor Ada and F. Isabel Campoy. Text copyright © 2004 by Alma Flor Ada and F. Isabel Campoy. Reprinted by permission of Disney/ Hyperion Books, an imprint of Disney Publishing Worldwide, LLC.

"Big Brown Moose" from *Winter Bees & Other Poems of the Cold* by Joyce Sidman, illustrated by Rick Allen. Text copyright © 2014 by Joyce Sidman. Illustrations copyright © 2014 by Rick Allen. Reprinted by permission of Houghton Mifflin Harcourt Publishing Company.

"The Cricket" (retitled from "El Grillo") from *También los Insectos son Perfectos* by Alberto Blanco. Text copyright © 1993 by Alberto Blanco. Translated and reprinted by permission of CIDCLI.

"Don't Touch Me!" by Elizabeth Preston from *CLICK* Magazine, October 2016. Text copyright © 2016 by Carus Publishing Company. Reprinted by permission of Cricket Media. All Cricket Media material is copyrighted by Carus Publishing d/b/a Cricket Media, and/or various authors and illustrators. Any commercial use or distribution of material without permission is strictly prohibited. Please visit http://www.cricketmedia.com/info/licensing for licensing and http://www.cricketmedia.com for subscriptions.

Drum Dream Girl (retitled from *Drum Dream Girl: How One Girl's Courage Changed Music*) by Margarita Engle, illustrated by Rafael López. Text copyright © 2015 by Margarita Engle. Illustrations copyright © 2015 by Rafael López. Reprinted by permission of Houghton Mifflin Harcourt Publishing Company.

Excerpt from *Experiment with What a Plant Needs to Grow* by Nadia Higgins. Text copyright © 2015 by Lerner Publishing Group, Inc. Reprinted with the permission of Lerner Publishing Company, a division of Lerner Publishing Group, Inc. All rights reserved. No part of this text excerpt may be used or reproduced in any manner whatsoever without the prior written permission of Lerner Publishing Group, Inc.

Goal! by Sean Taylor, photos by Caio Vilela. Text copyright © 2014 by Sean Taylor. Photos copyright © 2012 by Caio Vilela. Reprinted by arrangement with Henry Holt Books for Young Readers and Frances Lincoln, Ltd.

Web/Electronic Versions: *Goal!* by Sean Taylor, photos by Caio Vilela. Text copyright © 2014 by Sean Taylor. Photos copyright © 2012 by Caio Vilela. Reprinted by arrangement with Henry Holt Books for Young Readers and Frances Lincoln, Ltd. CAUTION: Users are warned that this work is protected under copyright laws and downloading is strictly prohibited. The right to reproduce or transfer the work via any medium must be secured with Henry Holt and Company.

I Am Helen Keller by Brad Meltzer. Illustrated by Christopher Eliopoulos. Text copyright © 2015 by Forty-four Steps, Inc. Illustrations copyright © 2015 by Christopher Eliopoulos. This edition published by arrangement and reprinted by permission of Dial Books for Young Readers, an imprint of Penguin Young Readers Group, a division of Penguin Random House, LLC and Writers House, LLC.

The Long, Long Journey (retitled from *The Long, Long Journey: The Godwit's Amazing Migration*) by Sandra Markle, illustrated by Mia Posada. Text copyright © 2013 by Sandra Markle. Illustrations copyright © 2013 by Mia Posada. Reprinted with the permission of Millbrook Press, a division of Lerner Publishing Group, Inc.

"May Day Around the World" by Tori Telfer, illustrated by Lynne Avril from *Ladybug* Magazine, Volume 20 Issue 5, May/June 2010. Text copyright © 2010 by Carus Publishing Company. Reprinted by permission of Cricket

Credits

333